Teaching
the NAEYC Code of Ethical Conduct

Stephanie Feeney, Nancy K. Freeman, and Eva Moravcik

Activity Sourcebook

National Association for the Education of Young Children
Washington, D.C.

National Association for the Education of Young Children
1509 16th Street, NW
Washington, DC 20036-1426
202-232-8777 or 800-424-2460
www.naeyc.org

Through its publications program the National Association for the Education of
Young Children (NAEYC) provides a forum for discussion of major issues and ideas
in the early childhood field, with the hope of provoking thought and promoting
professional growth. The views expressed or implied are not necessarily those of the
Association. NAEYC thanks the authors, who donated much time and effort to
develop this book as a contribution to the profession.

Library of Congress Card Number: 00-103765
ISBN 0-935989-95-1
NAEYC #118

Publications editor: Carol Copple
Editorial assistance: Lacy Thompson
Cover and book design and production: Malini Dominey

Printed in the United States of America

About the Authors

Stephanie Feeney is professor of education and early childhood specialist at the University of Hawaii at Manoa, where she is involved in undergraduate teacher preparation and graduate programs. She received her bachelor's degree at the University of California–Los Angeles, master's at Harvard University, and a Ph.D. at Claremont Graduate University.

Professor Feeney has been involved in early childhood policy formation, in Hawaii and nationally, for many years. She is a former member of the NAEYC Governing Board and its Ethics Commission and co-author of the NAEYC *Code of Ethical Conduct and Statement of Commitment* and *Ethics and the Early Childhood Educator: Using the NAEYC Code.* She also has served on the Governing Board of the National Association of Early Childhood Teacher Educators.

Professor Feeney has written and lectured extensively on children's aesthetic development, the impact of children's literature on social and emotional development, and ethics and professionalism. She is the author of numerous articles and several books, including the *Who Am I in the Lives of Children?* textbook, *Early Childhood Education in Asia and the Pacific: A Sourcebook,* a social studies curriculum for young children, and three children's books about Hawaii.

Nancy K. Freeman is assistant professor of early childhood education and research director of the Children's Center at the University of South Carolina in Columbia, where she teaches preservice teachers and oversees and facilitates research activities at the university's laboratory school. She received her bachelor's degree from St. Mary's College of Notre Dame, Indiana, and completed her master's and Ph.D. at the University of South Carolina.

Dr. Freeman serves on the NAEYC Panel on Professional Ethics in Early Childhood Education and has conducted research on teacher educators' use of the NAEYC Code of Ethical Conduct. She has been active in NAEYC on local, state, and national levels and has assumed leadership responsibilities in a number of other national and international professional organizations, including the Governing Board of the National Association of Early Childhood Teacher Educators.

In addition to her work on professional ethics, Dr. Freeman's published articles and research focus on issues of equity and diversity, particularly as they relate to preschool children and teacher education. She coauthored *Ethics and the Early Childhood Educator: Using the NAEYC Code.*

Eva Moravcik is assistant professor at Honolulu Community College, where she teaches early childhood education and coordinates the Leeward Community College Children's Center. She received her bachelor's and master's degrees from the University of Hawai'i.

Ms. Moravcik has been involved with advocacy, teacher training, teaching, and administration for many years and has been a teacher, program administrator, CDA (Child Development Associate) trainer, college professor, consultant, and workshop leader. She is a former president of Hawai'i AEYC and also has served as a member of NAEYC's Consulting Editors Panel.

Ms. Moravcik has written and lectured on many aspects of early childhood education, including documentation and observation, music education, aesthetic development, arts education, children's literature, curriculum planning, and social studies. She is an author of books and articles on early childhood education, including *Discovering Me and My World, Who Am I in the Lives of Children?* and *Hawaii ASK's.*

Contents

Preface

I believe in the importance of early childhood educators understanding ethics and knowing about the NAEYC Code of Ethical Conduct, but my undergraduate students' eyes glaze over when I start to teach about professional ethics

—College instructor

If I don't find a lively way to introduce ethics to my beginning students, I might as well just pass out sleeping pills at the door before I start to teach.

—College instructor

The teachers at my school are dedicated and hardworking, but they think that when I ask them to act professionally I'm inflexible and unfriendly. If I suggest inservice on ethics, they say they want something that is more practical and hands-on.

—Preschool director

When I present a workshop on ethics to early childhood teachers, the sessions turn into a group sharing of horror stories. I have a hard time helping people stay focused and see the big picture.

—Workshop presenter

As a person who provides training or supervision in the field of early education and care, you are aware that early childhood practitioners encounter many ethical predicaments in their work with children, families, and colleagues. You also know that it is important for them to be familiar with their ethical responsibilities and to use the Code of Ethical Conduct of their professional association, NAEYC.

This book, *Teaching the NAEYC Code of Ethical Conduct: Activity Sourcebook,* is designed to help you plan learning experiences that make the NAEYC Code come alive for early childhood educators in different settings and at different stages of professional development. Upon publication of a first book, *Ethics and the Early Childhood Educator: Using the NAEYC Code* (Feeney & Freeman 1999), we began planning and writing a second as a companion work to assist trainers, college teachers, program administrators, and other workshop leaders as they teach new and experienced early childhood educators about professional ethics and the NAEYC Code. This companion book was created as a resource to help educators in these positions use the first book and the NAEYC Code effectively in workshops, courses, and staff development activities.

The suggestions for teaching presented in this second book can be used with adult learners in a variety of situations. You may find them helpful if you are interested in initiating a dialogue about professional ethics in your center or school, if you are teaching preservice teachers and wonder how you can incorporate ethics into your already-full curriculum, or if you want to share your appreciation for the importance of the NAEYC Code at an early childhood conference.

Part 1 provides general guidelines and suggestions for teaching about professional ethics. The five sections of Part 2 describe teaching activities that can be used in courses and workshops. Part 3 offers some strategies for assessing student learning and evaluating teaching effectiveness.

Part 4 includes useful teaching resources. The first section contains 67 cases illustrating ethical dilemmas, keyed to the four sections of the NAEYC Code and formatted as case cards for easy use. A second section provides value choices as reproducible signs. The final section provides materials and directions for engaging students and participants in the Is It Ethical? game.

For general information about ethics and professionalism, we refer you to the references, recommended reading resources, and online sources for codes of ethics at the end of this book and to additional recommended readings in *Ethics and the Early Childhood Educator* (pp. 102–05).

We hope this book will be helpful to you in teaching about professional ethics and will enable the early childhood educators with whom you work to see the connection between the Ideals and Principles in the NAEYC Code of Ethical Conduct and their day-to-day work with children and families.

—Stephanie Feeney, Nancy K. Freeman, and Eva Moravcik

Acknowledgments

The writing of this sourcebook benefited from the work and support of many people. We thank Carrie Cheek for the suggestion that led to the writing of the book. We were fortunate to be able to draw on resources developed in Australia and Canada that related to teaching early childhood professional ethics. We were inspired to write our book by *Getting Ethical: A Resource Book for Workshop Leaders* by Lyn Fasoli and Chris Woodrow, written for the Australian Early Childhood Association. In addition we referred to *Taking Right Action: A Facilitator's Manual to the "Early Childhood Educators of British Columbia Code of Ethics"* by Sandra Griffen and Frances Ricks and *Will My Response Be Ethical? A Reflective Process to Guide the Practice of Early Childhood Students and Professionals* by Linda Newman and Lois Pollnitz, written for early childhood teacher educators in Australia.

Our thanks go to Sherry Nolte from Honolulu Community College for allowing us to adapt activities from the PACE 140 (Professional and Career Education for Early Childhood) program manual and to Cheryl Foster of Central Arizona College for sharing activities that she developed for teaching professional ethics. We have also drawn on materials developed with co-author Doris Christensen for the instructor's manual for the textbook *Who Am I in the Lives of Children?*

We gratefully acknowledge the interest and commitment of the members of NAEYC's Panel on Professional Ethics in Early Childhood Education who have given us valuable feedback for improving this book, with special thanks to Ethics Panel Chair Amy Driscoll for her encouragement and suggestions. We also wish to express our appreciation to NAEYC staff members Mary Duru and Polly Greenberg for their leadership of the Ethics Panel and Carol Copple and Millie Riley for their support of this project and attention to detail in the editing and production process.

And finally, we thank all of the early childhood educators who told us stories about the ethical issues they encountered in their work with children and families and Ken Kipnis for his continuing interest, support, and guidance.

I

Approaches to the Teaching of Ethics

Developing Plans, Strategies, and Activities

Everyone who works in a group setting with young children can benefit from training in professional ethics, although the characteristics of the participants will influence both the goals and teaching strategies for any course or workshop. As you plan your teaching, please keep in mind that the strategies and activities presented in this book are only suggestions. Adapt them according to the needs and characteristics of the group with whom you work.

In this Part 1 we discuss the goals for training, ways to accommodate learners' varied experiences, and some ways to plan for teaching.

Determine your goals

Before you begin designing your course, workshop, or training session, it is helpful to clarify your goals. Some goals for ethics training include helping learners

- become aware that ethics is an essential part of a profession and has special importance for early childhood educators;
- learn about ethics in early childhood education and the NAEYC Code of Ethical Conduct;
- develop a deeper understanding of the ethical dimensions of their work with children and families; and
- develop skills in identifying and analyzing ethical dilemmas.

You may choose one of these goals for a one-time workshop or several for a course, training session, or series of workshops.

Consider the learners

Early childhood educators know the value of providing learning experiences that match the needs and interests of the learner. This is as true in teaching adults as it is in teaching young children. Groups of individuals will react differently so you need to be sensitive and flexible in your approach, particularly when participants are new to the field or do not participate in the day-to-day care of young children.

Before you start to plan training, you will want to identify the characteristics of the learners.

- Are they beginners or veterans?
- What types of educational backgrounds do they have?
- What work experiences have they had?

Once you have considered these questions, you can think about what the learners might want or need to know about ethics and plan the learning experiences that you will use.

Brophy-Herb, Stein, and Kostelnik identify four phases of development in ethical understanding:

- *Awareness*. In the first phase individuals focus on the values that govern their lives, the values represented in their professional code, and the specific substance of that code.
- *Differentiating ethical judgments from other judgments*. In the second phase the individual emphasizes distinctions, figuring out what constitutes an ethical judgment and what does not.
- *Analyzing ethical dilemmas*. In phase three individuals apply methodological skills and strategies to the resolution of ethical dilemmas.
- *Applying the NAEYC Code in daily practice*. In phase four individuals learn how to translate ethical thinking into ethical conduct. (1998)

Working with beginning teachers/caregivers

The questions of early childhood education students and beginning teachers are immediate and concrete:

How do I get the children to pay attention to what I say?

What should I do tomorrow?

How do I create a peaceful, purposeful classroom?

How can I organize my work so that I get everything done?

How can I work effectively with the children's families?

The topic of ethics may not be real to students who are trying to gain mastery of practical teaching skills such as writing lesson plans, leading a group of children, or designing a learning environment. The ethical dimensions of an early childhood educator's work may not seem to be the most critical of issues to students or beginning teachers. Yet veteran early childhood educators know that learning about ethics is both an important professional responsibility and a valuable resource from the first days of one's teaching career.

If you work with students or neophyte teachers, your teaching task is first to develop their awareness of the ethical dimensions of working with children and families. After that you want to make the Code of Ethical Conduct come alive and help them see how it is relevant to their work. Your goal is to encourage in beginners a disposition to use the Code as a tool for identifying ethical responsibilities and for resolving ethical dilemmas.

Introductory courses or workshops usually devote limited time to teaching about professional ethics. In a 1996 survey of ethics instruction in preservice college classes, 61% of the respondents reported devoting three or fewer hours to teaching about ethics (Freeman 1996). It is reasonable, therefore, to assume that beginning teachers as well as students will have little familiarity with or expertise in approaching ethics. But in truth they may already be encountering ethical dilemmas.

Activities for these beginners must deliver content with power to make up the difference when a necessarily brief time is spent on ethics instruction. Throughout this book we indicate activities (✳) that are particularly effective with beginners because these

- do not require a great deal of experience or initiative,
- provide basic information,
- connect to and draw upon the learners' life experiences,
- make ethics real to the learner, and
- allow for active involvement that helps learners see the value of the NAEYC Code.

Working with experienced educators

Experienced early childhood practitioners will have mastered basic teaching skills and often have questions that have an ethical component:

How do I deal with a mother who asks me to do something I don't think is good for her child?

What can I do about a child in my class who often hurts other children?

Some of my colleagues are teaching in ways that I don't think are appropriate for young children. Should I say anything to them?

What should I do when a volunteer in my classroom asks me for information about a child's family?

The topic of ethics is likely to be very real to most experienced teachers, although they may not know that some of the issues they face involve ethics. For these teachers greater understanding of the ethical dimensions of their work and help in learning to address ethical dilemmas may be very meaningful. It will not be difficult to involve them in workshop or course content on ethics. They are likely to bring to the discussions many real-life experiences.

If you work with college students or experienced teachers, your first task is helping them acquire a strong foundation for understanding professional ethics. You will also want to help them develop skill in systematically addressing issues using the NAEYC Code and in clearly explaining their ethical positions.

In an advanced course or workshop, participants may already have had an introduction to ethics in their teacher education programs or through inservice training. These practitioners will be eager to share their experiences and will want solutions to issues that are confronting them. Activities for experienced practitioners must allow them time to share their experiences as they develop a deeper understanding of ethical dilemmas and skill in their systematic analysis.

Throughout this book we indicate activities (✶) that are particularly good for experienced practitioners because these

- let them share their professional experience,
- allow them to apply their professional experience,
- provide advanced information,
- help them develop skill in applying the Code,
- help them develop skill in ethical decisionmaking, and
- help them develop skill in justifying ethical decisions.

Staff who meet together on a regular basis will bring shared issues and experiences that the NAEYC Code can help them address. When there is a shared commitment to the profession's core values, weekly meetings that include open-ended explorations of ethical issues can be especially fruitful.

Working with varying degrees of experience

Any class, workshop, or staff may include both beginners and veterans with varying degrees of expertise and knowledge. Such diversity provides differences in perspective that can prove valuable as you help individuals expand their understanding of professional ethics.

You will find it helpful to ensure that in these groups you

- begin with an orientation to make certain that everyone has some basic ethics understanding;
- include real-life examples to make the topic come alive for everyone involved;
- allow time and structure groups that enable participants to share their experiences; and
- acknowledge what each participant contributes.

Plan to teach

Once you are clear on your purpose and have thought about the characteristics and needs of the learners, you can begin to plan your teaching. Consider how much time is available or how much time you can allot to the study of ethics. A one-time workshop raises awareness and gives basic information, while a series of sessions over a period of weeks or months allows opportunities for participants to read, reflect, and apply what they are learning.

As you begin to plan, decide what resources you want to use. If you are conducting a brief introductory workshop, you simply may call the group's attention to the *Ethics and the Early Childhood Educator* book and then make sure that each person has a copy of the NAEYC *Code of Ethical Conduct and Statement of Commitment* (Feeney & Kipnis 1998). Throughout the following pages we describe how to use the content of each chapter in the *Ethics* book to help early childhood students and practitioners understand and apply the NAEYC Code. If you are teaching ethics as part of a course or conducting a training series on ethics, it will be helpful to assign or make available copies of the *Ethics* book for all of the participants.

Regardless of the experience level of the group or the format of the training, we suggest that you

- begin with activities that build awareness (some introductory activities are described in the warm-up activities that follow);
- provide opportunities for participants to reflect on personal experiences (the reflection questions in each chapter of the *Ethics* book are good resources);
- choose activities that balance opportunities for taking in information in the form of reading or listening to a lecture with opportunities for expressing ideas and integrating new learning through active involvement such as discussion and games; and

• allow time for sharing personal experiences and concerns.

In a class or inservice training, you can help learners feel more prepared by assigning reading materials or a reflection assignment prior to the session.

Introductory activities

Adults, like children, need transitions that help them shift their focus and prepare for learning. A group of strangers need to establish a sense of comfort and trust. A group of students or colleagues who know each other well may need some time to greet one another before they can bring their attention to the topic of the session.

The activities that follow are designed to help your group of learners make the transition to the learning activities you have planned.

Sharing the purpose. Adult learners need to know the purpose of a session and what they can expect to feel assured their time will be well spent. It is a good idea to share a statement of purpose (verbally or on a chart or chalkboard) at the beginning of a session. Posting an agenda to give participants information about what you are planning to do is useful too.

Building a sense of trust. Because the discussion of ethics involves sharing personal feelings and experiences, it is important to build a sense of trust among members of the group. This is particularly important when participants are engaged in discussions of values, ethics, and appropriate and inappropriate professional behavior. Warm-up activities can contribute to the creation of a nonthreatening atmosphere in which participants feel comfortable enough to share freely without fear of criticism or judgment.

You may already have some warm-up activities that you use. We include a few of our favorites here.

Feeney, Freeman, & Moravcik

Activity 1: Match-Ups

Give everyone a list of questions, some related and some not related to the workshop topic (see example below). Participants fill in their answers, then try to find someone whose answer matches theirs.

When you were a child . . .	Your answer	Someone whose answer matches
What was your favorite toy?		
What was your favorite subject in school?		
What was your least favorite vegetable?		
How old were you when you first went to school?		
What embarrassed you the most?		
How many brothers did you have?		
How many sisters did you have?		
What was your favorite film or TV show?		
What was your favorite place to play?		
What did you want to be when you grew up?		
What did you think was the worst thing you could do?		
What were you afraid of?		

Activity 2: Scavenger Hunt

Give everyone a list of descriptive statements (see the example below). Participants interview one another to try to find someone who matches each of the descriptors. Participants sign their initials to each other's worksheets to create a record. They cannot directly ask questions of one another but must engage in conversations to find the answers.

If the participants are a group of people who know each other well, you might interview them in advance to learn unexpected things others might not know and then use these as descriptors (e.g., someone who took a college course on The Beatles, someone who knows sign language, and so on).

Find someone who . . .	Initials
is a cat lover	
is a dog lover	
grows a vegetable garden	
teaches three-year-olds	
went to high school in the 70s	
went to high school in the 90s	
performed in a musical	
likes to sail	
has served on a jury	
is the parent of a young child	
has lived in another country	
speaks a language other than English	
has read all the Narnia, Nancy Drew, or Harry Potter books or *The Wizard of Oz*	
has been president (of anything)	
likes to cook gourmet food	

Activity 3: Corners

Make a few statements that describe people or their personal preferences (individuals who love broccoli, people whose social security number starts with 5, anyone who has a brother). Ask participants to join a corner cluster of those who share this characteristic, exchange greetings, and start a conversation. After a brief time period, describe other personal traits and ask participants to move to another corner to form new get-acquainted clusters.

After allowing for several interchanges, call the groups together to begin your program.

Ground rules or agreements

When groups begin to discuss sensitive real-life situations, it is essential that you address the issue of confidentiality. It is also important to be aware of individual reactions. Steer participants away from judgmental behavior and statements.

Clearly laying out ground rules for the group at the outset helps prevent problems and is another way to build a sense of trust. We often post ground rules at the beginning of a session and ask the group to agree to them, add to them, or revise them. Here are our basic ground rules:

- Participate—there are many ways of participating, including listening to others.
- Honor other people's opinions and questions—no one will be put down or disregarded because of his or her opinions or questions.
- Maintain confidentiality—what is shared here will remain within this group and will not be discussed elsewhere.
- Pause after someone's comments to allow the group to reflect on them.

If we are teaching a college class, we add another rule:

- Handle problems responsibly with the person with whom you have the problem—don't complain to others or gossip. (We volunteer to serve as mediators if this is necessary.)

Other activities

Because adult learners come with prior knowledge, life experience, and a need-to-know, your teaching task is to make learning meaningful and be respectful of the learners' backgrounds. The activities you find in the sections of this book are designed to use the experience that learners bring and give them different ways to share their prior experiences with others. These methods include activities in which participants

- reflect (in conversations or writing) on situations they have encountered that have moral or ethical dimensions;
- think about ethics and their own experiences related to ethics through discussions or in writing;
- represent their experiences through drawing or writing;
- role play or dramatize their experiences;
- engage in games in which they make decisions and debate ideas; and
- analyze cases that involve ethics.

Reader reflections. The chapters in the *Ethics* book include reflection questions for participants to think, talk, or write about. (These are scattered throughout the book and are set off in bordered frames.) Most are useful even when people bring varying levels of experience in the field. Reflection questions can be used in different ways depending upon the makeup of your group and the purpose of your training session.

In a college class, use them as the basis for

- reflective writing in preparation for a class or after a class session,
- journal writing in class,
- the topic for class discussions, or
- written assignments.

In a workshop, the reflection questions provide

- an introduction to a topic and
- the impetus for discussion with a partner or small group.

For a staff inservice, these reflections serve as

- preparation for a staff meeting,
- an introduction to further reading, and
- topics for discussions.

Analyzing dilemmas. The Systematic/Reflective Case Study Method described in Part 2, "Teaching about Resolving Ethical Dilemmas" is a group process for working through dilemmas with participants who come with diverse experiences and expectations.

Closing a session

To conclude your work with a group, it is useful to clarify what has been done and relate the activities to the stated purposes. There are a number of ways to do this. Summarizing the session by making links between the purpose you shared at the beginning and what actually took place is one approach. You may also want to get feedback from participants to evaluate the workshop. Part 3 gives suggestions for doing this.

Learning about ethics is challenging and interesting. Participants, especially experienced practitioners, may come away from a session with an eagerness to continue exploring the issues and dilemmas raised. When this happens, you may work with the group to plan future sessions that probe ethics issues more deeply.

Exploration of Topics in Ethics

Teaching Morality and Ethics

(For use in teaching Chapter 1, *Ethics and the Early Childhood Educator*)

Early childhood practitioners who have had little or no experience with issues of professional ethics need some background information on the topic. They will benefit from learning experiences that help them develop necessary vocabulary and gain an awareness of personal values and morality and professional values and ethics. For those who have worked longer in the field and have some knowledge of professional ethics, providing learning experiences that build on this knowledge is a good place to start.

In the book *Ethics and the Early Childhood Educator,* Chapter 1 introduces the topics of morality and ethics. The chapter looks at the personal values and morality that early childhood educators bring to their work and at the core professional values and ethics they acquire in the course of their professional development. In this section we describe ways you can help participants in a course or workshop reflect on their personal values and morality and understand how these are similar to or different from professional values and ethics.

Personal values and morality

To a large extent, professional values and ethics are an extension of personal values and morality, so we begin with those topics. Activities that address personal values and morality allow participants to see that ethics is not terrifyingly abstract and has relevance to their lives.

To get group members into a frame of mind that helps them begin reflecting on their beliefs, you can start the workshop with one or two activities that make a link to personal values.

Activity 1. My Gift to Children

Start by asking participants to think about the children in their care and the one special gift they wish to give each child. Explain that the gift should be intangible (i.e., not a toy, material object, or resource such as money). It should be something they would like children to know, believe in, or be able to do.

Provide participants with crayons or markers and a handout titled "My Gift to Children." Below the handout's title heading, have a simple drawing of a plain box. Ask participants to write somewhere on the paper a description of the gift they envision. Next, ask them to use the markers to decorate the box.

When all participants finish their drawings, ask them to share their work individually with a partner or with the whole group. If the setting allows, post the drawings on the walls. Lead a discussion in which you help the participants reach the following conclusions:

- Each of the gifts has importance.

- Each individual has values that influence his or her work with children.

- There are similarities and differences in what we value for children.

Source: Adapted by permission, from S. Nolte, _PACE (Professional and Career Education for Early Childhood) Training Manual for ED 140,_ rev. ed. (Honolulu: Honolulu Community College, 1998).

Activity 2. The Wall of Personal Values

Label opposite walls of the room with signs saying, **Strongly Agree** and **Strongly Disagree.** Explain to the participants that the length of the room represents a continuum of personal opinion.

Read aloud several statements that reflect values, and with each statement ask participants to walk to a place along the continuum that best represents the extent to which they agree or disagree.

Start with statements that represent perspectives on personal values and morality that are likely to cause little conflict or difference. Gradually move to other statements that present more challenges for the group. As the activity progresses, note any body language that suggests discomfort. Although some discomfort is useful, too much may prevent participants from engaging in further activities. Some examples of statements you could use are given in the box that follows.

> - It is better to do good than to be wealthy.
> - It is more important to be smart than to be good or moral.
> - It is OK to lie under certain circumstances.
> - Following your own conscience is more important than doing what others want you to do.
> - It is important to follow the law even if you disagree with it.
> - It is OK to steal if your family really needs something.
> - Family responsibilities are more important than your responsibilities to yourself or your employer.
> - People need formal religious institutions such as churches to help them determine what is right and wrong.
> - Society does not have the right to dictate how people will raise, care for, or educate their children.
> - As a society we have the right and responsibility to ban harmful substances and devices such as drugs and guns.
> - As a society we have the responsibility to make sure that all peoples' needs for food, shelter, and medical care are met.
> - No price is too great to preserve our environment.
> - It is never OK to take a life.
> - Gay marriage should be legalized.

After participants have responded to a few personal values statements, spend some time talking with the group. Comment that there were similarities and differences within the group and there may have been some surprises when individuals discovered some people had feelings quite different from their own.

Ask the group to discuss the experience—what they had expected and what they found surprising. Note that all of the sample statements reflect values. Ask these questions: Is it possible for two people to be good professionals even if their personal values are very different? Why?

Variation 1. Instead of having participants physically moving to a position of agreement/disagreement, have them mark their position along a continuum on a worksheet. In small groups compare the positions individuals take.

Example statement: It is better to do good than to be wealthy.

Strongly Agree				Strongly Disagree

Variation 2. Ask participants to create their own values statements. Then repeat the process.

Activity 3. Sources of Values

Ask participants to make a list of 10 to 15 ideals, principles, qualities, accomplishments, actions, circumstances that they value most. If you wish,

What I value	Source of the value
❏ education	
❏ beauty	
❏ religion	
❏ competence	
❏ creativity	
❏ doing good	
❏ excitement and stimulation	
❏ family	
❏ financial well-being	
❏ friendship	
❏ happiness	
❏ honesty	
❏ health	
❏ intellectual curiosity	
❏ meaningful work	
❏ the natural environment	
❏ order	
❏ peace	

Feeney, Freeman, and Moravcik

provide a prepared list similar to the one on the opposite page on which participants may check, add, or eliminate ideas. When the lists are finished, have the participants indicate the source (person or people, institution or experience) for each value in their own lives.

With the total group, compile a list of the sources of personal values and discuss why individuals' values may have different sources.

Variation on "Sources of Values." To the created lists add a third column headed with the word *Action.* For each value, have participants write an action they take in their lives that grows out of that value. Working as partners or all together in the larger group, discuss how values influence our lives and work.

Activity 4. Values Auction

Create a collection of values signs (see "Value Choices" in Part 4 for 36 signs you can duplicate). Make enough signs for an active auction—a number two to three times the size of your group. Give each participant $100 in play money. To begin the auction, explain that with this money participants can bid on values that you have for sale. Show them the values signs. In turn, hold up each value choice that is for sale. Participants bid and buy until all the value choices are sold.

When the auction concludes, ask the participants what they noticed about themselves during the bidding and how strongly they felt about different values. Next, ask the group what differences they noticed in participants' bidding and buying. Lead a discussion that helps individuals see that diverse backgrounds and experiences cause people to have different values or to value some things more highly than others.

Activity 5. Reflection on Personal Values

Have participants think about and then write or discuss their ideas on the following values reflection from the *Ethics* book, Chapter 1, page 5.

> *Identify some personal values that have led you to choose a career working with young children. Think of some things you do with children and families that reflect these values. Think about a teacher who has positively influenced your life. What personal values did that teacher demonstrate?*

Activity 6. What Would You Do?

Ask participants to reflect on what they would do in a variety of situations involving personal moral choices. In small groups have participants explain what they would do and why and what influences in their lives lead them to believe these are moral choices.

Some sample situations you might read to the group appear below.

The mom-and-pop store. You go to a neighborhood mom-and-pop grocery and give a ten-dollar bill for a $3.50 purchase. You take your change and walk out. Outside the store you realize that the cashier (the mom) has given you change for a twenty-dollar bill. What would you do?

The chain discount store. You go to an outlet of a nationwide chain discount store and use a charge card to pay. When you get your credit card bill you realize that you were charged $9.95 for an item that cost $39.95. What would you do?

The towel. You are staying in a hotel that has nice, thick towels. On the day you plan to leave, you go for a swim and return to your room to pack. Your bathing suit is wet, and there are no plastic bags. If you don't wrap your bathing suit in something, you will ruin your clothes. What would you do?

The water playground. Your friend is the lifeguard at an exclusive club that has an elaborate water playground. Members are identified in the water with a special bracelet they wear. Your friend offers to give you a bracelet so that you can go any time you want. What would you do?

The special party. The day of the event is approaching. You accept an invitation from someone who is romantically interested in you even though you're really not interested. The next day the person you most wish would ask you out invites you to the party. What would you do?

The dented fender. You're backing your car out of a tight space in a parking garage. You hear a crunch and realize that you have hit the car next to you. You get out and see that there is a small dent in the side of the brand-new car. No one saw you. What would you do?

Activity 7. Which Is Right?

Give pairs of participants matched statements that describe two opposing points of view, each of which could be justified as being right (see examples below). Ask the first person to share and justify her or his position for a minute or two, then switch sides and have the other partner give a justification for the opposing viewpoint. Continue with several pairs of statements.

Bring the pairs together in the larger group and invite them to discuss what they conclude from the experience with regard to moral dilemmas. Introduce the idea that right-versus-wrong choices (responsibilities versus temptations) are very different from right-versus-right choices (dilemmas).

It is right to protect the old growth forest and the endangered spotted owl.	It is right to provide jobs for loggers.
It is right to honor a woman's right to make decisions affecting her body.	It is right to protect the lives of the unborn.
It is right to provide all our children with the finest public schools available.	It is right to prevent the constant increases in taxes.
It is right to provide equal social services to everyone regardless of race or ethnic origin.	It is right to pay special attention to those whose background has denied them opportunities.
It is right to refrain from meddling in the internal affairs of sovereign nations.	It is right to help protect the undefended in warring regions where they are subject to slaughter.
It is right to resist the importation from developing nations of products made to the detriment of their environment.	It is right to provide jobs, even at low wages, for citizens of developing nations.
It is right to condemn the minister who has an affair with a parishioner.	It is right to extend mercy to a minister who has made a serious mistake.
It is right to take your family on a much-needed vacation.	It is right to save vacation money for your children's education.
It is right to support creative and aesthetic freedom in art.	It is right to avoid displaying pornographic or racially offensive work.
It is right to speak up in favor of a minority viewpoint.	It is right to let the majority rule.

Source: Adapted by permission, from R.M. Kidder, *How Good People Make Tough Choices* (New York: Fireside, 1995), 16.

Activity 8. Reflect on Morality

Have participants reflect on and write about or discuss the following reflection questions from the *Ethics* book (Chapter 1, p. 6).

What are some of your strongly held ideas about morality? Where or from whom do you think you acquired them? Reflect on the experiences in your life that led you to develop these views of morality.

Activity 9. Children's Literature Connections

As a way to introduce a topic or bring closure to a session, we often read a children's book that relates to or illuminates a topic. When teaching about morality and ethics we have read

Red is Best by Kathy Stinson or *Bread and Jam for Frances* by Russell Hoban to discuss how personal preferences are different from values;

Bare Naked Book by Kathy Stinson to explore personal values;

The Empty Pot by Demi to illustrate personal morality; and

Song for the Ancient Forest by Nancy Luenn as an example of an ethical dilemma.

Professional values and professionalism

Awareness of personal values and morals can lead to an understanding of professional values. The following activities are designed to help participants become aware of professional values, see how these differ from personal values, and develop an understanding of the characteristics of a profession.

Activity 10. The Wall of Professional Values

Label opposite walls of the room with signs: **Strongly Agree** and **Strongly Disagree** (see "Activity 2" described on p. 18). Explain to participants that the length of the room represents a continuum of personal opinion about professional values.

Read to the group statements that reflect professional values. Ask participants to walk to the place along the continuum between the walls that best represents their viewpoint about a given values statement. Some of the types of statements you might use with the group follow.

- A teacher's most important task is to help children feel good about themselves.
- Children who attend preschool and kindergarten should learn the discipline they will need later in school.
- Children won't learn unless the teacher tells them what to do.
- Development of intellectual skills is the most important task of an early childhood program.
- Given enough time and equipment, children will learn all they need without traditional, formal teaching.
- Children should be allowed to play in school.
- Families should not be allowed to interfere in their child's schooling.
- To be fair, all children should be treated the same way in school.
- It is important for teachers to be responsive to the individual needs and interests of all children.
- It is appropriate for educators to use rewards to help change children's behaviors.
- Early childhood curriculums should be based on what children will need to know in later schooling.
- Children who misbehave should not be allowed special privileges.
- It is important for children [choose an age group] to learn to color within and cut on the lines, write neatly, stand in line, and use proper punctuation.

Variation. Instead of having participants physically move to locations between the walls that represent their opinions, have them mark their positions on worksheets (see the example on p. 20). With a partner or in small groups, individuals may compare and discuss their responses.

Activity 11. Reflect on Professional Values

Using the following reflection from the *Ethics* book (Chapter 1, p. 8), have participants work with one or two partners to explore their thinking.

> *Brainstorm a list of values that you think all early childhood educators should hold. Compare your list to the list of Core Values in the NAEYC Code of Ethical Conduct. Consider why these lists are similar to each other or different.*

After the small groups brainstorm, bring the larger group together again and discuss why their lists are similar to or different from each other's and how core values form a foundation for the profession's Code of Ethical Conduct. Invite the participants to reflect silently on the Code's Core Values and their personal reaction to and commitment to each one as you or someone from the group reads them aloud.

Activity 12. What Makes a Profession?

Ask participants to name two or three jobs they regard as professions. If they need help, give them some examples such as politician, real estate agent, engineer, secretary, nurse. Participants are likely to express a variety of opinions. Some may believe that anyone who gets paid for work is a professional, and others may say that only certain extensively trained individuals have earned professional status.

Guide the group by explaining that you are looking for occupational titles that everyone agrees are professions. Once this list is established, form small groups and ask each participant to brainstorm characteristics that these professions share.

When the groups report back, share their lists of pro and compare these to those on the opposite page, which studying the literature describing professions.

Use the profile on the opposite page to segue into a discussion on ethical codes: What professions have codes and why and how are the codes used?

- A profession requires practitioners to participate in *prolonged training* based on principles that involve judgment for their application, not a precise set of behaviors that apply in all cases.

- Professional training is delivered in accredited institutions. Rigorous *requirements for entry* to the training are controlled by members of the profession.

- A profession bases its work on a *specialized body of knowledge and expertise*, which is applied according to the particular needs of each case.

- Members of the profession have agreed on *standards of practice*—procedures that are appropriate to the solution of ordinary predicaments that practitioners expect to encounter in their work.

- A profession is characterized by *autonomy*—it makes its own decisions regarding entry to the field, training, licensing, and standards. The profession exercises internal control over the quality of the services offered and regulates itself.

- A profession has a *commitment to serving a significant social value*. It is altruistic and service oriented rather than profit oriented. Its primary goal is to meet the needs of clients. Society recognizes a profession as the only group within the community that can perform its specialized function.

- A profession has a *code of ethics* that spells out its obligations to society. Because the profession may be the only group that can perform a particular function, it is important for the public to have confidence that the profession will meet its obligations and serve the public good. A code of ethics communicates the unique mission of a field and assures that services will be rendered in accordance with high standards and acceptable moral conduct.

Source: Reprinted from S. Feeney and N.K. Freeman, *Ethics and the Early Childhood Educator: Using the NAEYC Code* (Washington, DC: NAEYC, 1999), 7.

Activity 13. Debate—Is Early Childhood Education a Profession?

After the group explores the characteristics of a profession, help participants deepen their personal understanding of the meaning of *profession* by holding a debate. Form teams of three or four persons (ensure an even number of teams). Ask the teams to pair up, assigning sides of *for* or *against*. Debate the question: Is early childhood education a profession?

Ethics

Ethics and codes of ethical conduct are related to professional values. The activities that follow are designed to help participants build their awareness of ethics and a knowledge of the nature of ethical codes.

Activity 14. Ethics in the News, in the Comics

Whether you're teaching a workshop or a course, you will want to help participants realize that issues of morality and ethics come up often in our society. An effective way to kick off an introductory workshop or conference session is by sharing newspaper headlines related to ethics and morality. They don't have to relate to schools or teaching.

Whatever the specific topic, newspaper stories help participants realize they need a foundation in ethics—it's a topic that affects their everyday lives.

Start your collection by keeping an eye out for headlines in your local newspaper. Our collection of headlines includes

"Marines look for the few, the strong, the ethical"

"Schools teach ethics and ABCs"

"I don't think it's very ethical to do a child this way" (a quote from a story about a teacher who wrote a reminder on a kindergarten child's arm)

"Teen ethics: More cheating and lying"

"48% of workers admit to unethical or illegal acts"

"Doing the wrong thing"

"Ethics for teachers needed"

Think about some ways to introduce your session using overhead transparencies or enlargements of recent headlines similar to these. Another source for illustrating the pervasiveness of ethical issues is the comics section of the newspaper. The comic strips *Garfield*, *Peanuts*, *The Family Circus*, and others often address values, morals, and ethics. Like newspaper headlines, comic strips help an audience appreciate the ethical dimensions of their everyday interactions with children and adults alike.

Activity 15. Why a Code of Ethics?

Why is it important for a profession to have a code of ethics? Divide the workshop or class into small groups to brainstorm some answers to this question. Have the groups report back and compare their responses. Emphasize the following points:

- Professionals are doing a job that is essential to the society.
- Professionals are the only ones who can do a particular job.
- Professionals monitor themselves (no one else tells them what to do).
- It is essential, therefore, that the profession as a whole agrees that its members will conduct themselves according to high moral standards.

✸ Activity 16. Codes of Ethics Study

Give small groups of participants copies of codes of ethics from other fields (e.g., psychology, nursing, special education, elementary/secondary education) along with NAEYC's *Code of Ethical Conduct and Statement of Commitment* (see "Online Sources for Codes of Ethics," p. 114). Encourage participants to work together to find similarities and differences between the various codes. Reconvene the total group and have representatives from the small groups report the similarities and differences they noted in the codes. Discuss whether they noticed any unique characteristics of the NAEYC Code.

Variation. Compare codes of ethics for early childhood educators from other nations (e.g., Australia, Canada [British Columbia]) with the NAEYC Code. Discuss why there are differences and what this suggests about practice in different places (see "Online Sources for Codes of Ethics," p. 114).

✸ Activity 17. Read/Teach about Ethics

Refer participants in your workshop, inservice, or class to the "Recommended Reading" in the *Ethics* book (pp. 102–05) to further their learning about professional ethics. These resources also may help you to design brief lectures on ethics and professionalism.

Teaching the NAEYC Code

(For use in teaching Chapter 2, *Ethics and the
Early Childhood Educator*)

Every professional early childhood educator needs an awareness of the NAEYC Code of Ethical Conduct and an understanding of how it is used and why. We have found that only more experienced professionals who have a serious commitment to early childhood education have enough background to understand the importance of the development of the Code and an interest in the issue of enforcement. Chapter 2 in *Ethics and the Early Childhood Educator* discusses the need for a code of ethics for early childhood educators and the history of the development of the NAEYC Code. It also provides an overview of the Code and a discussion regarding the issue of its enforcement.

If you are doing an introductory workshop, you may choose to touch lightly upon or skip sections on history and enforcement in order to move from an introduction to values, morality, and ethics into an engagement with ethical dilemmas.

The NAEYC Code

Because beginners usually do not have a high need-to-know about the history of the NAEYC Code or the issues of enforcement, in this section we begin by describing some ways you can help the participants in a course or workshop to understand the features of the Code.

If you are conducting a course or series of nonintroductory workshops, have students read the Code and Chapter 2 in *Ethics and the Early Childhood Educator* before beginning the activities.

✳ Activity 1. In Other Words

In this activity participants make a poster to summarize the ethical principles for one section of the Code. If you are doing this with a group that meets regularly, assign a read-through of the Code as homework. The procedure follows.

- Divide into small groups of two to six individuals. Assign each small group the task of reading one section of the Code. "Ethical responsibilities to children" may be broken down into two parts, P-1.1 to P-1.4 and P-1.5 to P-1.9. "Ethical responsibilities to families" may be broken down into two parts, P-2.1 to P-2.6 and P-2.7 to P-2.11. "Ethical responsibilities to colleagues" may be broken down by sections on co-workers, employers, and employees. "Ethical responsibilities to community and society" may be broken down into two parts, P-4.1 to P-4.6 and P-4.7 to P-4.11.

- Give one sheet of chart paper and a set of colored marking pens to each small group. If you have time in advance, write at the top of the sheets of chart paper, "Our responsibilities to (children, families, etc.) are to . . . "

- Explain that each group is to summarize in one to three sentences the big ideas for its section of the Code. Remind the groups to focus on the ethical "Principles" (the musts and must nots) rather than the "Ideals" (the aspirations). When the groups have completed their tasks, ask each to write and illustrate its sentences on chart paper and post it on the walls or bulletin boards of the room.

- When all the posters are up, "walk through" the work that has been done, pointing out that each section of the Code has some important ideas that are guiding principles for our work with children. This is a good opportunity to emphasize what is critical about the Code, gently note what has been missed or mistaken in the presented work, and point to Principle 1.1 as the overriding principle of our work with children.

Variation on "In Other Words." Sometimes the prospect of understanding the responsibilities we have to the multiple clients identified in the Code can seem too large a task. If you sense that the participants with whom you are working would benefit from a more focused and less comprehensive approach, concentrate on just one section at a time.

- Select one section that seems most relevant to the group: responsibilities to children, families, colleagues, or community and society.

- Download the Code from NAEYC's Website (www.naeyc.org/about/position/pseth98.htm). Cut apart the Code, distribute a section of it to participants, and try "Activity 1. In Other Words," thus limiting your focus.

Feeney, Freeman, and Moravcik

✳ Activity 2. Ethical Code Puzzle

A puzzle can encourage participants to actually read the words of the Code. It helps participants see the Code as a whole, like a completed jigsaw puzzle.

Make the puzzle.

- Print out a copy of the Code of Ethical Conduct beginning with Section 1 (available online: www.naeyc.org/about/position/pseth98.htm). Remove the titles and numbers from all the sections so that all you have left is the written text.

- For each group of participants, make a copy of the altered Code, and cut it apart so that for each group you have a set of pieces that includes

  1. each of the "Ethical responsibilities" sections with titles removed,

  2. all the "Ideals" sections with the numbers removed and cut apart into two or more segments, and

  3. all the "Principles" sections with the numbers removed and cut apart into two or more segments.

How to play.

- Divide participants into small groups.

- Have participants of each group sort the pieces of the game into piles that go together.

- Give participants pieces of paper or index cards and ask them to label each pile, or give participants labels with the titles from the Code ("Section 1: Ethical responsibilities to children," etc.) and ask them to place the label with the correct pile.

Variations. Create different degrees of difficulty by including or eliminating parts of the Code.

Source: Activity suggested by Cheryl Foster, Central Arizona College, Coolidge.

✪ Activity 3. In My Experience

In this small-group activity, participants share and discuss their experiences related to a single Principle in the NAEYC Code of Ethical Conduct. By focusing in this way, participants find relevance that is often lost in trying to decipher the entire Code.

Preparation.

- Copy the NAEYC Code from the *Ethics and the Early Childhood Educator* book (or use the online version). Cut out the individual Principles.

- Place several Principles (these need not be related or from the same section of the Code) in an envelope on a table for a small group of participants. Be sure to include at least one Principle that relates to a common situation (for example, divorce—P-2.10; child abuse—P-1.6; or concerns about a co-worker—P-3A.1) as well Principles related to more uncommon situations.

What you do.

- Form small groups and have participants of each group open their envelope and select a Principle.

- Ask them to think of and discuss specific classroom situations they have encountered in which they have had to apply this Principle.

- Explain that if they can't think of an example, they should move on to the next Principle.

- Ask each group to report to the larger group.

- Lead a group discussion that focuses on the big picture of Ideals, Principles, and the Code of Ethical Conduct in its entirety.

Source: Activity by Cheryl Foster, Central Arizona College, and suggested for inclusion in this book.

✳ Activity 4. Is It Ethical?

In this activity (developed by Eva Moravcik), participants play the Is It Ethical? game (see Part 4 for materials) in which they use the NAEYC Code of Ethical Conduct to explore whether an action is ethical or is not ethical. Make one set of the situation cards for each small group (we make sets in different colors to make sure that we can reassemble them easily). If you are doing this with a group that meets regularly, assign participants to read the Code as homework.

Starting the game.

- Give each group a set of the cards and the instructions.

- Randomly distribute the cards describing ethical dilemmas and a tally sheet to each member of the group.

- One player reads a dilemma aloud to the group.

- Players silently decide whether the response is ethical or not ethical and write **E** or **NE** on their tally sheets without showing one another.

- Each player then tells the group why she or he thinks the answer is or is not ethical.

- All participants look through the Code for the ethical Principle (or Principles) that supports their decision.

- Members of the group discuss what they have found, and each person writes next to his or her decision on the sheet the Principles he or she thinks are most applicable. It is OK for players to change their decisions after hearing about the discoveries of the other group members.

- Continue with as many situations as possible until time is called.

Ending the game.
- Get all participants' attention.

- Explain to all that if they were able to use the Code and make connections between their ethical choices and the Code's Principles, they are winners.

- Have the players use the master sheets and their own experiences with the Code to review the ethical situations described and talk about the Principles that apply. Note that in some situations the Code indicates clear *ethical responsibilities,* while at other times it helps us to identify *ethical dilemmas.*

- Discuss how the Code might be used in real-life situations and why its existence is important to the profession.

★ Activity 5. Reflection on the NAEYC Code

Have participants work with one or two partners to react to the following reflection questions from the *Ethics* book (Chapter 2, p. 19).

> *How did you first learn about the NAEYC Code of Ethical Conduct? What was your initial reaction to it? How have you used it in your work? In what ways have you found it helpful?*

After the small groups have talked, reconvene the large group and discuss how the NAEYC Code can be helpful to early childhood educators.

Why is a code of ethics important?

More experienced practitioners are often aware of the recurring ethical issues that arise in practice. Next in this section of our sourcebook, we provide activities that help practitioners examine the value of the Code in their own practice and in the field of early care and education.

✳ Activity 6. The NAEYC Code and Me

Invite two or three experienced early childhood professionals with an interest in the NAEYC Code to sit on a panel. Ask the members of the panel to respond to questions such as the following:

- How did you learn about the NAEYC Code of Ethical Conduct?
- How have you used the NAEYC Code of Ethical Conduct at different points in your career?
- What kinds of ethical issues and dilemmas come up regularly in your daily work?
- In your experience what kinds of ethical responsibilities and dilemmas are most difficult to deal with for beginners? For more experienced practitioners? Why?
- How has the NAEYC Code of Ethical Conduct been helpful to you in addressing these dilemmas?

✭ Activity 7. Code/No Code

Select some of the difficult dilemmas from Part 4, "67 Selected Cases." Duplicate these and make them into cards. Give several cards containing dilemmas to small groups of participants. Have each group discuss how a practitioner or program would handle the situation without a code of ethics for guidance. Then ask the group to discuss how the dilemma might be addressed with the help of the NAEYC Code of Ethical Conduct. Have the participants respond to the following questions:

- Why do early childhood educators need a code of ethics?
- What would happen if there were no code?
- How does having a code of ethics improve the status of the early childhood education field?

Have a representative from each small group report back to the large group.

✷ Activity 8. Reflection on the Need for a Code of Ethics

Have participants work with one or two partners to read the four points supporting the importance of a code of ethics and consider the following reflection questions from the *Ethics* book (Chapter 2, pp. 12–15). (If the group is not using the book, provide a handout with the four points.)

> *Do you think that the four foregoing points discussed provide a strong case for the need for a code of ethics for the early childhood field? What experiences have you had with each one that support your view? Are there other aspects of the early childhood education field that suggest the need for a code of ethics?*

After the small groups have talked, reconvene as the large group and ask volunteers to share their views about the most compelling reasons for having the Code of Ethical Conduct in early childhood education and care.

The issue of enforcement

The activities that follow can help groups who are interested in the issue of enforcement to explore some of the factors involved. These activities are most appropriate for people who have had a lot of experience with the Code or as a follow-up session for those who wish to learn more about how the NAEYC Code is implemented. More experienced practitioners may have strong feelings about whether the Code should or should not be enforced.

✷ Activity 9. Reflection on Code Enforcement

Have participants work with one or two partners or in a small group to respond to the following reflection questions from the *Ethics* book (Chapter 2, p. 20).

> *What would be the advantages of enforcing the NAEYC Code? What are the advantages of having it be voluntary? Which do you think is preferable and why? Do you think it is desirable to require everyone who works with young children to demonstrate a knowledge of the Code and skill in applying it? What might be some disadvantages in this requirement?*

After small groups have talked, bring them together in the large group and discuss how an enforced code of ethics would differ from a voluntary code and the advantages and disadvantages of each.

☆ Activity 10. Debate on Code Enforcement

This activity can be used with any group of fairly confident and articulate participants. The formal debate imposes a structure that ensures coverage for both sides of the issue. If you are meeting with a group more than once, this activity could be set up ahead of time to allow participants to prepare their arguments.

Procedure.

- Select two small groups of debaters (three to four people in each group).

- Pose the questions (stemming from the preceding reflection activity): Why is enforcement of the NAEYC Code a good idea for the early childhood field? Why is it not a good idea? One group of debaters will argue the position, "Yes, the NAEYC Code of Ethical Conduct should be enforced." The other group will support the opposing position, "No, the NAEYC Code of Ethical Conduct should not be enforced."

- Ask each group to summarize its arguments.

- Point out the major issues that emerge from the debate.

Teaching about Ethical Dilemmas

(For use in teaching Chapter 3, *Ethics and the
Early Childhood Educator*)

Examination of the ethical dimensions of early childhood education in Chapter 3 of *Ethics and the Early Childhood Educator* helps those who work with young children learn to distinguish between ethical responsibilities and ethical dilemmas. Understanding this distinction is important. This section offers suggestions for ways you can help workshop or course participants learn to identify their ethical responsibilities, distinguish between ethical responsibilities and ethical dilemmas, and use a basic approach to analyzing ethical dilemmas.

Ethical responsibilities and ethical dilemmas

Ethical responsibilities, the things that the good professional will always do or always refuse to do, are clear-cut and spelled out in the NAEYC Code of Ethical Conduct. For example, Principle 1.1 makes it clear that the good early childhood professional would refuse to hit a child even if instructed to do so by a supervisor or parent. Although following through on an ethical responsibility may be difficult, identifying the ethical responsibility is relatively easy. Your goal in teaching is to help learners use the Code to identify these clear-cut ethical responsibilities and to help them to distinguish between personal preferences and morality and professional ethical responsibilities.

Ethical dilemmas, however, are situations in which two or more different responses can be defended by NAEYC's Code. For example, concern for the needs of the child and respect for the needs and wishes of the family make a dilemma of the situation in which a parent asks the teacher not to allow her child to nap. Each choice in an ethical dilemma has costs and benefits and reflects an ethical principle.

Not every dilemma faced by early childhood educators is an ethical dilemma. For example, the dilemma of whether or not to expend scarce resources for teaching materials or to save them for future use is certainly a dilemma, but it does not have ethical implications. Your goals in teaching about ethical dilemmas are to help learners develop the skill to identify issues that have an ethical component and to make the distinction between ethical responsibilities and dilemmas.

✳ Activity 1. Do's and Don'ts

This activity is similar to "Activity 1. In Other Words" in the previous section ("Teaching the NAEYC Code"). If you have already used that activity, you may want to simply refer to it instead of repeating the first procedure below, which is similar.

Procedure 1.

- Divide participants into small groups, one for each section of the Code. (If participants in your course or workshop have different professional roles, you could use these as the basis for assigning the groups—teachers, assistant teachers, directors, etc.)

- Give each group a set of marking pens and a piece of poster paper folded in lengthwise to make two columns. Write, or direct participants to write, **Do's** at the top of one column and **Don'ts** at the top of the second column.

- Give the groups the task of creating a list of rules for early childhood educators based on one section of the NAEYC Code. (Give an example: Don't hurt children physically or mentally.) As each group finishes, have members display their poster where it can be seen by all.

- Review the posters with the large group to make sure everyone understands what each of the small groups meant. Clarify and simplify the wording if necessary and make sure nothing major has been omitted or added.

- Tell the participants that they have created a list of an early childhood educator's *ethical responsibilities*.

Procedure 2.

- Give each group a page or two of descriptions of problem situations (some examples are included in the chart on the next page, but you will want to supplement this list, and if using it as a handout, remove the given Code notations) in which an early childhood educator might need to make a choice. Include some situations involving ethical responsibilities and others that simply involve common teaching problems.

- Using the posted list of responsibilities, have groups identify the problems that involve ethical responsibilities and those involving a teaching decision.

✳ Activity 2. Responsibility or Dilemma?

Select a number of ethical cases from Part 4 ("67 Selected Cases"), including some that involve ethical responsibilities (such as 2.6, 2.9, 2.18, 3.25, and 4.1) and some that include ethical dilemmas (such as 2.1, 2.2, 2.4, 2.8, 3.11, 3.21).

Read aloud each case (or provide participants with case cards). Ask participants to form pairs to decide whether a case is an example of an ethical responsibility (for which the Code gives specific and unambiguous guidance) or an ethical dilemma (in which the practitioner must make a choice between two supportable choices).

Invite the participants to share their conclusions and explain how they arrived at them. Repeat the activity with other cases.

Source: Adapted by permission, from L. Fasoli and C. Woodrow, *Getting Ethical: A Resource Book for Workshop Leaders,* vol. 3 (Watson, ACT: Australian Early Childhood Association, 1991).

✳ Activity 3. Which Is Right?

To introduce the concept of a moral or ethical dilemma, use "Activity 7. Which Is Right?" in Part 2, "Teaching Morality and Ethics."

Problem situations	Ethical responsibility?	Teaching decision?
1. A family asks you to discipline their child by spanking.	(P-1.1)	
2. The director recommends that you give up hugging the children to avoid being accused of sexual abuse.		
3. You have a child who cannot participate in holiday activities because of religious beliefs. You have always had a class Halloween party and a week of activities to get ready.	(P-1.2)	
4. You need to call a meeting to decide whether or not to get special help for a child who is not making progress. Who's invited?	(P-1.4)	
5. A child says he hates art and will never participate in art activities.		
6. A child comes from home displaying bruises and says her daddy hit her because she wet the bed.	(P-1.5)	
7. You discover that the teacher in the next room is using a highly toxic insecticide in her classroom while children are present.	(P-1.9) (P-3A.1)	
8. An obnoxious parent asks if he can come and sit in your class for a day to see how his child does in school.	(P-2.1)	
9. A parent tells you she doesn't like the way you tell stories and thinks you should use more flannel boards.		
10. One of the parents in your school is arrested, and the account of his arrest is on TV. A friend asks you to tell her about the family.	(P-2.9)	
11. The teacher in the next room sings off-key and only knows five songs.		
12. A prospective parent asks you if you teach the children to read. If you say no, she may not bring her child to your school.	(P-4.1)	
13. You're asked to take two additional children into your room even though that will put you over the maximum number allowed by state licensing.	(P-4.8)	

Feeney, Freeman, and Moravcik

✳ Activity 4. Reflect on a Dilemma

Have participants write their thoughts and reflect silently or work with one or two partners to respond to the following reflection questions from the *Ethics* book (Chapter 3, p. 27).

> *Have you ever been in a situation in which you were forced to choose between two alternatives that both seemed desirable? What were the competing interests? How did you respond? How did you know if that was the right thing to do?*

After individuals have reflected and small groups have talked, reconvene the large group and discuss the nature of dilemmas.

Activity 5. Whose Dilemma Is It?

Select a number of ethical cases from the first section in Part 4, that are clearly ethical dilemmas (such as 2.1, 2.2, 2.4, 2.8, 3.11, 3.21).

Read aloud each case (or provide case cards). Have participants work in pairs to decide what the dilemma is and whose dilemma it is.

Invite participants to share their conclusions and explain how they came to them. Repeat the activity with other cases.

✳ Activity 6. Real-Life Dilemmas

Have participants work in small groups and ask them to recall a dilemma they have experienced in their work with children and families. Invite several individuals who are comfortable doing so to share a dilemma, discuss how they resolved it, and give the rationale that guided their resolution. Ask each group to answer the following questions:

- Was the situation an ethical dilemma?
- What made it a dilemma?
- What are some other supportable resolutions based on the NAEYC Code?

✷ Activity 7. Reflection on an Ethical Dilemma

Have participants write their ideas and reflect silently or work with one or two partners on the following set of reflection questions from the *Ethics* book (Chapter 3, p. 23).

> *Consider a situation that tempted you to do what was easy or popular rather than what you believed was right. What did you do? Were you able to keep sight of your responsibilities to children, families, and colleagues? How would you describe your decisionmaking process to someone new to the field?*

After individuals have reflected and groups have talked, bring participants together in the large group and discuss how the Code might have helped them deal with the dilemma. (If you are working with a group of beginning practitioners, you might want to ask them to discuss a personal rather than a professional ethical dilemma.)

✷ Activity 8. Is It Ethical? Game

This game (see Part 4 for materials) is described in the previous section ("Activity 4," pp. 34–35) and with the help of the Code is useful in helping participants develop skills in identifying and addressing ethical dilemmas.

If you have not played the game with the group before, use the instructions described in the previous section "Teaching the NAEYC Code." If participants have played it before, ask them to go back to the game, this time sorting the cases into responsibilities versus dilemmas. Then ask participants to identify at least two ethically supportable responses to each dilemma and an ethical Principle from the Code that supports each response.

✷ Activity 9. Ethical Pursuits Game

Select cases (see "67 Selected Cases" in Part 4). Make a set of response cards headed with **Ethical, Not Ethical,** and **It Depends.** Create just enough cards so that each participant has only one of the three responses. Have participants work in small groups of four or five. Distribute a case card and response card to each participant.

The purpose of this exercise is not to resolve the dilemma but rather to practice taking an assigned perspective when facing an ethical issue.

Feeney, Freeman, and Moravcik

Procedure.

- Each player reads aloud his or her case and then defends the position described on the response card he or she holds. Other members of the small group challenge the argument.

- Following this same method, each participant presents his or her case.

Remember to allow enough time so that each player can have the spotlight. It may be necessary to remind participants to move on to the next player when they become too engrossed in lively conversations.

Debrief participants after this activity by discussing how, in addressing dilemmas, it is possible to identify more than one ethically supportable position. While we may not agree with each position, it is possible to defend or argue the point of view because it is supported by NAEYC's Code of Ethical Conduct.

Source: Adapted by permission, from L. Fasoli and C. Woodrow, *Getting Ethical: A Resource Book for Workshop Leaders,* vol. 3 (Watson, ACT: Australian Early Childhood Association, 1991).

Addressing dilemmas

The steps in resolving a dilemma are outlined in the *Ethics* book (Chapter 3). To help participants become familiar with ethical decisionmaking, select an ethical dilemma and walk participants through the process of

1. exploring the issue (determining that it is an ethical dilemma and identifying the relevant sections of the Code);

2. making an initial effort to resolve the dilemma by finding a resolution without winners and losers (ethical finesse);

3. deciding on a course of action when ethical finesse does not work; and

4. revisiting and reflecting on the decision, the course of action, and possible implications for policy.

✫ Activity 10. The Flow Chart

As you work with groups of participants on a hypothetical or actual dilemma, use the flow chart (*Ethics* book, p. 25) to guide the group through the steps, from identifying an ethical dilemma to resolving it.

✴ Activity 11. Three Approaches

Choose one of the 10 cases from the *Ethics* book. Read it aloud or have participants read it silently. Invite participants to consider the resolution to the case offered in the book in terms of the three philosophical approaches to ethics also described (*Ethics* book, p. 28). These can be summarized using the following questions:

- Is this resolution best for the greatest number of people?
- Is this resolution the most moral or right action? Is this what all early childhood educators should do?
- Does this resolution reflect how I would I want others to treat me?

✴ Activity 12. Reflection on Resolving a Dilemma

Have participants write about and reflect silently or work with one or two partners to explore the following reflection questions from the *Ethics* book (Chapter 3, p. 33).

> *Think about a time when you made a hard decision regarding an ethical dilemma. Who were the stakeholders, and what were your obligations to each? What resources did you use to help you resolve the dilemma? What was the outcome, and was it successful?*

After individuals have reflected or small groups have talked, bring the large group together and discuss how having a clear outline of the process of resolving a dilemma (outlined in the flow chart in the *Ethics* book, p. 25) might have helped them. Encourage them to identify the aspects of the dilemma that could still be difficult to address despite having such a tool.

This might be a good time to get participants thinking about and discussing why ethical dilemmas are so difficult to resolve.

Teaching about Resolving Ethical Dilemmas

(For use in teaching Chapters 4–7, *Ethics and the Early Childhood Educator*)

In this section we describe a number of teaching strategies that you can use to help participants in your courses and workshops learn to resolve ethical dilemmas. We hope they will help you support early childhood educators in their efforts to become more proficient at honoring their responsibilities to children, families, colleagues, and community and society—the constituencies our NAEYC Code of Ethical Conduct identifies.

All of the activities in this section involve participants in the process of addressing realistic cases. Many of the cases come from our own experience or were shared with us by early childhood educators. Others are adapted from professional ethics resources developed by the Australian Early Childhood Association (AECA).

Using cases

Presenting topics in the context of particular problems facilitates teaching about ethical responsibilities and dilemmas. You probably agree, for example, that it is easier to think about Timothy and his mother's request that he not take a nap (*Ethics* book, Chapter 5, Case 3) than to remember a prioritized list of rules about how to weigh one's responsibilities to a variety of stakeholders. What's more, a case based on a true situation retains the ambiguity of real life. We seldom encounter clear-cut, easily described problems, but instead we have to think carefully about the facts to discern the ethical issue imbedded in many ordinary day-to-day interactions.

Effective cases are always good stories. They can be as long as a short book or as brief as two or three sentences. This book includes a collection of cases (see

Part 4) describing situations that are familiar to anyone who has spent time working with young children and their families. The cases present situations that make early childhood educators struggle to answer the question, What should the good early childhood educator do?

This collection of cases is a good place to begin. It's likely, however, that you and the early childhood educators with whom you work will be able to describe real-life dilemmas you both have faced in your work. These stories also become useful resources for learning how to understand and resolve ethical dilemmas.

Ground rules

Several important ground rules will help your work with cases go well. First, keep in mind that cases are simply tools to help you teach ethics effectively. Feel free to modify them as needed. You might want to add additional facts to a case to make an important point or clarify an event or interaction.

Second, when conducting ethics workshops, never use the name of any person or program that might be recognized by anyone in the group. Public discussions of situations with ethical dimensions must always honor the confidentiality that comes with your professional responsibilities.

Finally, it is critically important that you create a safe setting for potentially revealing conversations about ethics. All discussions should begin with a clear statement that you will respect participants' contributions, and, in turn, you expect them to demonstrate consideration and respect for each other. What's more, your discussions as well as the content of the cases should be held in confidence, for they are likely to elicit strong emotions and reactions.

The Systematic/Reflective Case Study Method

We begin with a technique that is useful when you have sufficient time to work through a dilemma in some depth. The Systematic/Reflective Case Study Method developed by Nancy Freeman (1997) illustrates how an early childhood practitioner can work through an ethical dilemma. This process can be effective whether you are leading an ethics workshop for a center's staff members who have an ongoing relationship; teaching a university or community college class for which students are together a semester; or presenting a conference session that engages participants who share an interest in learning more about professional ethics. The same process can be used to resolve real problems in the workplace and the hypothetical dilemmas used during workshops and training sessions.

The process has seven steps and includes individual reflections, small-group discussions, and large-group synthesis.

Step 1: Introduce the scenario. Read the case carefully (out loud if possible) and ask participants to write down their first reactions. Then ask them to put aside this initial, intuitive response and not share it with anyone.

Most participants react immediately to a difficult situation by jumping to a solution. Many early childhood educators who read about Timothy (Case 3, Chapter 5 in the *Ethics* book), for example, are inclined to react to his mother's request that he not take a nap without giving the situation much thought. It's true that for most dilemmas it is easy to come up with a response that seems workable almost immediately.

Have participants keep their written responses to themselves. You will ask them to revisit these after they work through the process of addressing ethical situations deliberately.

Now small groups of three to five persons should work together to find their best solution to the dilemma. Using broad markers on large chart paper (or transparencies), record each group's responses so that their insights can be shared during the large-group debriefing process.

Small-group discussion is an important part of debriefing. It's our experience that participants who are reluctant to speak out in a large group often are willing try out their ideas with three or four peers. This opportunity for an individual to explain his or her position seems to bolster many participants' confidence, making many more willing to add their perspectives to large-group discussions.

Steps 2 and 3 correspond to the first step of the process used to analyze the cases (see "Explore the issue," pp. 38–39 in the *Ethics* book). They help the participants to identify the people involved in the situation.

Step 2: Determine the players. Make a list identifying everyone who cares what happens in the case (the stakeholders). Invariably the problem expands beyond just those three or four individuals directly involved. Before long an entire classroom, often the whole school, and frequently the larger community are identified as stakeholders.

When groups discuss Timothy's case, for example, it's obvious that Timothy, his mother, and the teacher are interested in finding a resolution to the problem. But before long, participants may consider how this situation affects Timothy's classmates and their families, the other teachers, and the program's administration. Making a list of players can be a lengthy process, but it's an effective way to begin small-group discussions.

As participants identify all the players in any dilemma, they begin to gain insights into the complexity of teaching and the connections that link children, families, homes, schools, and the community. It's interesting how useful it is for both inexperienced preservice students and experienced practitioners to observe the frequency with which problems expand beyond one classroom's four walls.

Step 3: Determine each player's investment. Each player brings a unique perspective to the situation. Why does a particular individual care? What issues involve and affect each person?

When we think about Timothy, some of the issues that emerge are his teacher's responsibility to meet the needs of all children, her desire to be responsive to parents' concerns, and considerations of teachers' autonomy and professionalism. Linking each player to one or more issues makes the complexity of the case apparent.

Step 4: Brainstorm solutions without evaluating them. When participants begin brainstorming resolutions, making no effort to evaluate the merits of their suggestions, discussions are apt to become lively and spirited. At this point you may want to suggest that participants consult the NAEYC Code. It will remind them to consider all stakeholders' perspectives and may bring additional alternatives to mind. The brainstorming process should generate as long a list of alternatives as possible, including out-of-the-box creative approaches.

In an effective brainstorming session, a way may emerge for the stakeholders to finesse the problem. That is, participants may think of solutions that don't require a hard, moral choice but are compromises that are acceptable to all. This discovery will highlight the usefulness and potential of ethical finesse. Solving problems through careful conversation and negotiation can be satisfying and is often preferable to having to take a hard-line position.

Think of the solutions we considered in Chapter 5 of *Ethics and the Early Childhood Educator* in which we discussed the nap case. Timothy's teacher explored the possibility of moving him to another classroom where the children don't nap; she suggested that the mother find a neighbor or relative willing to wear him out before dinner; and she asked the mother to try making some changes in his bedtime routine, hoping that might solve the problem. She might even have considered letting Timothy nap but telling his mother he didn't. These are the kinds of solutions that are likely to emerge during the brainstorming process.

Participants often report that brainstorming makes them appreciate the different perspectives colleagues and peers bring to their work. In fact, many individuals are surprised that others propose solutions that are very different from those that had occurred to them. Assuming an uncritical perspective at this point is important. Each participant needs to know his or her suggestion will be accepted without critique. We have observed that this assurance is likely to encourage even reluctant speakers to participate in this essential part of the debriefing process.

Step 4 corresponds to the second step (see "Make an initial effort to resolve the problem," pp. 40–42 in the *Ethics* book), which is also used in *Ethics* Chapters 5 to 8.

Step 5: Identify solutions that are acceptable to ethical early childhood professionals. The brainstorming process is likely to generate an extensive list of solutions to the problem, including more approaches than any one person could have thought of on his or her own. Now it's time to hold the Code up to the alternative solutions and determine which pass muster and which fall short of the NAEYC Code's Ideals and Principles for our profession. Also, participants who have been ready to entertain compromise must be prepared to take a firm stand when efforts to finesse the problem are not successful or appropriate.

Returning to Timothy's story, we might be able to resolve the problem by using one of the approaches identified in Step 4. The majority honor the responsibilities identified in the NAEYC Code. One idea suggested, however, is not acceptable. We could not let Timothy sleep but tell his mother that he didn't! If we were to accept that alternative, we would be violating our responsibility to "involve families in significant decisions affecting their child" (P-2.4).

Testing solutions against the Code is a critical component of this Systematic/Reflective Case Study Method. There would be no point in ethical decisionmaking if every alternative were acceptable. After all, it's the ability to differentiate the good solutions from bad ones that makes it so important for early childhood educators to learn to apply the NAEYC Code.

As workshop participants decide how they would resolve a particular problem, they are likely to realize there are several defensible solutions to complex ethical dilemmas. Choosing between those acceptable alternatives may be difficult, and in many instances the choice between two or more alternatives is a matter of personal preference. Our goal is to help early childhood educators avoid making unethical choices, ones that may be popular or expedient but which do not honor their responsibilities to children, families, colleagues, or the community and society. Identifying the wrong answers and avoiding ethical missteps are important reasons for learning about professional ethics.

Step 5 corresponds to the third step we used in approaching the cases in the *Ethics* book (see "Decide on a course of action," pp. 41–42).

Step 6: Large-group case debriefing. When small groups have finished working through this systematic process, it's time to compare notes. By this time all of the participants should have added their voices to their group's discussion, and everyone's ideas should have been acknowledged during the process of generating lists of players, issues, and acceptable resolutions. The large pieces of chart paper or overhead transparencies provide a record of the small-group discussions. We find it helpful to tape chart papers to the walls or show transparencies on an overhead projector so that everyone can see evidence of each group's deliberations.

As we review the notes together, participants have the opportunity to learn from each other. In our experience most participants contribute to these large-group discussions, even those who are usually reserved. Having the chance to try out their ideas in the small, safe setting seems to help even generally quiet individuals feel confident that they have good ideas to contribute.

Reaching a large-group consensus is not always an easy process. And, in reality, more than one acceptable resolution is likely to emerge when informed professionals are working on a difficult dilemma together. Workshop participants often report that both the small-group and large-group discussions exposed them to a variety of alternatives they would never have considered on their own, which also demonstrates the value of collaboration. They see the truth in the saying that two [or more] heads are better than one.

Step 7: Look back at your initial response. After the large-group debriefing session, it's instructive to revisit the off-the-top-of-one's-head solutions participants jotted down after they read the problem for the first time. Did their approaches to the case change in the process of carefully considering the people and issues involved? Did brainstorming with peers help them see complexities and dimensions of the problem they might overlook if they were trying to solve it alone? Has this exercise helped them see the value of working with peers toward finding an answer to the question, What would a good early childhood educator do? and grounding their decision in the NAEYC Code of Ethical Conduct?

We have found that this approach helps slow down the process of resolving ethical dilemmas, builds in opportunities for reflection, and helps even novices appreciate the complexities of their work and the value of collaborative problem solving. These insights are valuable not just when early childhood practitioners address problems in workshops, conferences, or class sessions but also when they confront real-life dilemmas in the early childhood settings where they work.

Role plays

Role-playing activities make the words on the page come to life, as participants become involved in making hypothetical situations become more real. The situations give individuals experience interacting with each other, responding quickly, and thinking on their feet. When role plays require participants to take a position that is not necessarily their own, the experience is likely to increase the players' sensitivity to differences and empathy for the position of another.

Feeney, Freeman, and Moravcik

The role-playing activities that follow can be lot of fun. They also may be threatening if not sensitively handled. Participants need to be comfortable with each other. They must be willing to risk going out on a limb, taking an unpopular stance in assuming an assigned persona. Particular care must be taken to allow participants who have assumed an unpopular position to come out of that role completely before moving on to another activity.

It may be helpful to have props that define particular roles: a clipboard for the teacher; a walkie-talkie for the director; a hat, jacket, or car keys for a parent. These reminders might make it easier to take on and step out of various roles and make transitions from one role to another.

The activities that follow are likely to be more effective in workshops with colleagues or in college classes than in professional conference sessions in which participants do not know each other.

Debriefing is an essential part of the role-playing process. Make sure that you give participants plenty of time to reflect and discuss what went on in the role play, feelings experienced in the different roles, and what they learned.

✮ Activity 1. Ethical Pursuits

If you have not already engaged participants in the Ethical Pursuits game (see "Teaching about Ethical Dilemmas" in Part 2, Activity 9 on p. 44), it provides a lively and nonthreatening introduction to role-playing ethical issues.

✮ Activity 2. Performance Role Plays

Performance role plays require participants to be actively involved and present challenges beyond those in the Ethical Pursuits game. Players experience a situation very personally and have the opportunity to become aware of their own reactions and positions. When conducting a performance role play, give players an opportunity to leave their assigned personas behind and become themselves before moving on to the next activity or discussion.

Procedure.
- Provide or generate a situation involving an ethical dilemma.
- Assign participants to play the part of each major role. Others coach the actors during the "performance." This support makes it less stressful for the performers and keeps all participants actively involved.
- After the role play ask all participants to respond to the arguments and positions presented and discuss the issues raised during the reenactment.

Variations. Depending on group members' confidence and experience, it may be more effective to divide the large group into several teams. Ask each team to assign a player for each role and appoint a recorder. Then have each team work through the same dilemma. After the small-group reenactments are complete, reconvene the large group and give each team's recorder an opportunity to report the main arguments discussed.

This format works well because players are asked to work only with a few peers. That means they are likely to be more spontaneous and less anxious than they would be playing to a large group. What's more, this variation involves everyone in the debriefing process.

✶ Activity 3. Hypothetical Hyperethicals

Each participant takes a role and explores not only the actions but also the feelings and attitudes of a specific stakeholder in an ethical dilemma. As the facilitator, you will need to carefully identify all conceivable stakeholders before the role-playing begins. Plan conscientiously and think through all predictable arguments so that you can effectively set up the role play.

Procedure.
- Select an ethical dilemma from the cases in Part 4 or from your own experience.
- Involve participants in listing all the individuals who could possibly be considered stakeholders.
- Gather participants to form a large circle and explain that you are going to ask each person to put aside his or her own perspective and assume the values, priorities, and interests of the assigned role.
- Start by explaining the background of the dilemma and assigning each individual a role. For example,

  Jane, you are a teacher in the Kids Corner center in a small town in your state. A friend who is visiting from a nearby city tells you she knew one of your co-workers who used to work at the center, which her child attended. Your friend tells you that your colleague was fired from that center for suspected child abuse. You are going to work the next day, and you have to decide what, if anything, you will say to your director.

  Next, choose a center director, a parent who is worried about child abuse, a social worker, and so on. You can add details that require a response if

Feeney, Freeman, and Moravcik

participants are being overly cautious, or you can invent more stakehold-ers, create additional incidents, or modify the scenario in any way that will require participants to face critical issues and clarify their positions.

- As the facilitator you also can use the Code to challenge participants to consider the mandates of specific sections that relate to the issue.
- When the players have thoroughly explored all actors' feelings, attitudes, and actions you can stop the activity and discuss the dilemma and the issues it has raised in a more detached and objective way.

Variation. A more elaborate version of this activity is to actually stage the play by assigning roles in advance, giving participants an opportunity to prac-tice their parts, and present the performance as a staff-development exercise or a class session.

Role-play reminders

Remember that workshop leaders always need to be sensitive to individu-als' characteristics when leading groups through role plays. They need to be ready to make the challenge appropriate, neither too stressful and complex nor too straightforward and obvious. They also need to help participants see the usefulness of the exercises, for sometimes the process becomes the focus rather than the attitudes, knowledge, and skills that are your objective when you are teaching ethics.

Source: Activities 1, 2, and 3 adapted by permission, from L. Fasoli and C. Woodrow, *Getting Ethical: A Resource Book for Workshop Leaders,* vol. 3 (Watson, ACT: Australian Early Childhood Association, 1991), 6–9.

Other activities

Observations and panel discussions provide additional experiences for students and inservice professionals to develop skills and a variety of perspectives.

✵ Activity 4. Ethics Observations

If you work with preservice teachers involved in practicums, internships, or student teaching, keep a log of situations you observe that have moral and ethical dimensions. In seminar meetings share these observations, inviting students to add additional information about the dynamics of particular sce-narios. Ask students to turn to the Code to find the rationale that could help them (or the master teachers with whom they work) take a difficult stand or resolve a dilemma successfully.

It is important to remind students to honor confidences and hold these sensitive discussions in strictest confidence.

★ Activity 5. Experts Panel

This activity is designed for a large class, workshop, or conference session. Invite professionals from a variety of disciplines, all of whom have an interest and expertise in ethical dimensions of child and family issues (e.g., an early childhood educator well versed in the NAEYC Code, a lawyer specializing in family law; a social worker familiar with custody and/or abuse issues; and a cleric who counsels in family services settings) to participate in a panel discussion of ethical dilemmas.

A week or so before the panel presentation, provide each participant with two or three dilemmas that relate to his or her areas of expertise. For example, you could use a case that requires a professional to differentiate between child abuse and culturally accepted disciplinary practices and another that describes the dilemma a teacher in a religious school faces when she finds that her colleague is working at a topless bar to earn extra money. Be sure that each person has enough information to feel prepared and confident.

When the panel convenes, read a dilemma to the group and ask each of the panel members to describe the priorities and values that would guide his or her decisionmaking. The purpose is not to debate or decide on one best answer. It is to help participants understand the perspectives, values, and priorities of professionals from varied disciplines and to help them to see that professionals can prioritize their responsibilities differently and come to diverse resolutions for the same ethical dilemmas. In fact, this exercise has the potential to expose not just the participants but also the panel members involved to some unfamiliar perspectives that might help them to understand each other better.

Since this is a labor-intensive project and depends on the cooperative efforts of representatives from a number of disciplines, you will want to be sure you have sufficient numbers of participants to make it a worthwhile investment of everyone's time and effort. One of the authors of this book implemented it successfully at a statewide AEYC leadership conference, and it was instructive.

Teaching the Code
As a Living Document

(For use in teaching Chapter 8, *Ethics and the
Early Childhood Educator*)

We suggest that you conclude your study of ethics by helping
college students and workshop participants see how professional ethics has
influenced and continues to influence our field. Having access to the NAEYC
Code of Ethical Conduct and Statement of Commitment (Feeney & Kipnis 1998) and
learning how to use the Code are just the first steps to ethical competence. In
our earlier book, *Ethics and the Early Childhood Educator,* Chapter 8 highlights the
field's ongoing efforts to make explicit the ethical dimensions of early childhood educators' work and to put professional ethics in the spotlight.

The Code isn't playing its intended role if we get a copy, focus on it for a
little while during a workshop, class, or conference session, for example, and
then file it away with other so-called important papers that often aren't really
very useful. The Code comes to life when individual practitioners at every stage
of their professional careers rely on it to develop, refine, and reexamine their
understandings of what the good early childhood educator should do.

The activities in this section highlight the progress that has been made
in bringing attention to the importance of ethics in early childhood education since the publication of the first NAEYC ethics survey in 1984. We hope
these activities help your students see that ethics is indeed alive and well in
early childhood education. We also want to point out that there is much
more we all can do.

Awareness of professional ethics

Even if you have just a short time to focus on ethics, you will want to equip your students or workshop participants with information about how they can share with others their enthusiasm for and interest in ethics and the NAEYC Code of Ethical Conduct.

✳ Activity 1. Where Can I Find the NAEYC Code?

The Code is readily available, but do students know how to get it? Make sure that everyone knows where to find a copy of the Code and encourage all to share it with friends, colleagues, or the families of children in their programs.

Pose the question, "Where can you get a copy of the NAEYC Code?" as you begin your wrap-up activities. Have readily available these details about how to get copies:

- It is included in the book *Ethics and the Early Childhood Educator.*

- NAEYC prints the Code in brochure form in English (#503) and Spanish (#504) versions.

- It is available online through the NAEYC Website as a position statement (www.naeyc.org/about/position/pseth98.htm).

Activity 2. An Ethics Quest

We say that ethics has assumed a more prominent role in our professional conversations, but how can we demonstrate this is the case? Have students or workshop participants conduct an ethics quest to find out for themselves who is talking about and writing about ethics.

You might have the resources needed to complete this assignment on the shelves in your office for workshop participants, or students can visit the library to find the answers to these questions. It will be helpful for them to observe firsthand the growing interest in ethics.

Early childhood textbooks. Look at early childhood textbooks (it is best if you have older and newer editions of the same text).

- Does this book mention the NAEYC Code of Ethical Conduct?

- Does it quote from the Code?

- Does it include some or all of the text of the Code?

Feeney, Freeman, and Moravcik

- Does a discussion of ethics stream through the book, or is ethics an isolated topic?
- Is the coverage of ethics increased in this book's most recent revision?

Have students or participants discuss what they learn.

Early childhood journals. Examine copies of NAEYC's journal *Young Children.*

- How many articles addressed ethics in the past year?
- How many articles addressed ethics five years ago? Ten years ago?
- Examine other journals written for teachers of young children. Do students or participants see any articles or features devoted to professional ethics?
- If any students or participants work in elementary settings, include a look at elementary education journals as well.

Have students or participants discuss what they found.

Professional conferences. Save the programs of local, regional, and/or national early childhood conferences that you attend. Ask your colleagues to add to your collection.

- Are there ethics sessions addressed to teachers and caregivers?
- Are there ethics sessions addressed to directors or administrators?
- Are there sessions addressed to leaders preparing to teach ethics?

Have students or participants discuss what they find.

✳ Activity 3. Ethics in the News

There is no better source than your local newspaper for close-to-home stories that demonstrate ethics is an ongoing issue.

It's sad but true that every community periodically hears about a child care provider or teacher who has made an ethical misstep. Your local paper might include headlines about a director who violated child care regulations for facilities or a teacher who belittled or abused a child in the name of discipline.

There also may be accounts of courageous and successful teachers and caregivers who were effective advocates for young children and our profession. Their success stories may report that child care regulations have been changed to require lower adult-child ratios or that legislation has been passed that supports children, families, or early childhood educators.

- Have students or workshop participants watch their local media (news-papers, magazines, television, and radio) for stories about teachers, early childhood education, or child welfare. Have them clip (or collect over time) articles and bring them to the workshop or class. If you have space or a bulletin board, you could display them.

- Analyze the data they bring in or collect to see if ethics is involved and in what ways. Have them think about how the Code could have helped some individuals avoid such headline-grabbing attention or empowered others to use their voices on behalf of children who cannot speak for themselves.

✴ Activity 4. Add Your Voice to the Conversation

NAEYC's Panel on Professional Ethics in Early Childhood Education (referred to as the Ethics Panel) has a series in *Young Children*, "Using the NAEYC Code of Ethics." It often includes an ethical dilemma and asks for readers' responses. Include an article from this series in your ethics work-shop or course if the timing is right.

Have participants or students use "The Systematic/Reflective Case Study Method" process given in the previous section (pp. 48–52) to work through a case and reach a well-reasoned, carefully articulated response. Submit the rationale to *Young Children* in time to be included in a future article. Think how empowering it would be for your students or workshop participants to see the results of their deliberations published!

The Ethics Panel is continually exploring ways to involve NAEYC members in conversations about professional ethics. Stay informed about their ongoing efforts by reading *Young Children* and checking the NAEYC Website.

✴ Activity 5. Is It Really Unethical?

Without thoughtful consideration of an ethical issue, we risk trivializing the Code or casually evoking its authority. We need to be cautious, for example, that we don't use the Code to justify our position whenever we encounter something that we object to or disagree with.

It can be tempting, for example, to claim, "That's unethical," when we really may be questioning the actions of a colleague, supervisor, or employee based on our knowledge of best practice. It's not always easy to decide on the most ethical course of action and, likewise, it is not always easy to identify issues with ethical dimensions. Caution and thoughtfulness are in order (Stonehouse 1994).

Have participants in your course or workshop think about situations in which they have heard someone say, "That's unethical!" After you have brainstormed some examples, classify the responses into concerns that actually do have ethical dimensions and those that are differences of opinion about best practice. You can take this analysis one step further and differentiate between ethical dilemmas and situations that involve ethical responsibilities.

If you will meet with the participants again, have them watch for this expression, "That's unethical!" and record those instances when they hear it used and the circumstances they observe.

☆ Activity 6. Add Ethics to Other Conversations

As Anne Stonehouse (1994) points out, sometimes policy and opinion leaders in our communities are the sharpest critics and detractors of early childhood care and education. Demonstrating our reliance on a professional statement of values and ideals may help skeptics appreciate the specialized knowledge base that is the foundation of our work, thus making our efforts on behalf of children and families more effective.

If participants in your workshop or students in your class hold leadership positions in the community or are in a position to influence lawmakers or shapers of social policy, the following exercise can prepare them to take advantage of opportunities that may arise to share the Code outside the early childhood profession.

- Brainstorm a list of all the groups in your community/state who work on behalf of children and families and who might benefit from knowing about the NAEYC Code. Discuss how this knowledge might be beneficial to children and families.

- Discuss all the ways you can think of to reference the Code or incorporate it into programs and policies related to the welfare of children and families (NAEYC Ethics Panel 1995).

✴ Activity 7. Creating New Guidelines

When the NAEYC Code was developed in the late 1980s, the decision was made, due to a lack of resources, to focus only on the dilemmas faced by those who work directly with young children on a day-to-day basis. The ethical issues of early childhood educators who have other responsibilities (including program directors, early childhood teacher educators, and licensing workers) were not explicitly addressed.

If some participants or students work in these arenas, they will bring a firsthand knowledge of that work and are likely to have insights that will make this exercise beneficial.

- Identify a group of early childhood educators whose dilemmas are not addressed in the NAEYC Code.
- Identify the constituencies to whom those practitioners have ethical responsibilities.
- Identify the commonly occurring situations in their work arena that have ethical dimensions.
- Reflect on professional values, principles, and ideals that could help them weigh their conflicting responsibilities.

Activity 8. The Personal and the Professional Intertwining

The person you are influences your professional work, and your profession influences the person you are. It's true that ethics is a cyclical process, changing individuals and their work together.

Have your students or the participants of a workshop think about and discuss these reflection questions from the *Ethics* book (p. 98).

> *How do you think your work in early childhood education has affected your personal values and morality? How has the Code influenced your thinking about what is right and wrong in working with young children and their families? Does knowledge of the NAEYC Code of Ethical Conduct change your feelings about the value of the work you do? Has the Code contributed to your sense of being a professional?*

After discussing the questions in a small group, writing in their journals, or writing response papers, volunteers may share their insights with the entire group. These reflections may be very personal, so you will want to approach this final exercise with particular sensitivity to the sentiments expressed.

Assessment and Evaluation

Determining Our Success
in Ethics Teaching

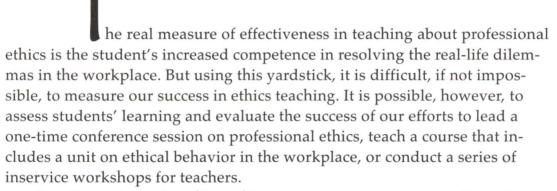

The real measure of effectiveness in teaching about professional ethics is the student's increased competence in resolving the real-life dilemmas in the workplace. But using this yardstick, it is difficult, if not impossible, to measure our success in ethics teaching. It is possible, however, to assess students' learning and evaluate the success of our efforts to lead a one-time conference session on professional ethics, teach a course that includes a unit on ethical behavior in the workplace, or conduct a series of inservice workshops for teachers.

Two dimensions of teaching ethics—assessment of participants' learning and evaluation of teaching effectiveness—are the focus of this section. When you teach a session on ethics, you will want to determine if the learners gained the knowledge, skills, and dispositions that you hoped they would as a result of your time together. You will also want to judge the effectiveness of your format, presentation techniques, and activities. Did the participants in your session, class, or workshop think that their time was well spent and that you helped them to think clearly about the ethical dimensions of their work?

Your approach to gathering this information and how you measure success will depend on the particular circumstances of your work. We offer these suggestions to help you consider how to approach the task.

Assessing learning

What did you want participants to take from the conference session, class periods, or seminars you devoted to ethics? To answer this question you to need to revisit the goals that guided your efforts.

Was it your intention to raise conference participants' awareness of the NAEYC Code of Ethical Conduct so that they would pursue future opportunities to study and practice its application? Were you aiming to make preservice teachers sensitive to the unique responsibilities resting upon the shoulders of those who work with young children and to help them realize they will face ethical issues that do not have clear-cut, easily reached resolutions?

Were you providing an inservice workshop for a center's staff to give a foundation for ongoing professional discussions of the ethical dimensions of their work together? Or were you perhaps focused on helping graduate students become adept at articulating their processes of ethical decisionmaking? Effective evaluation begins by revisiting your objectives and thinking about how you will know if you achieved them.

Surveying participants

Even if you have a limited period of time to lead a conversation about ethics, as you would if you were presenting a conference session, you will still want to encourage participants to reflect upon your presentation and identify what they have learned.

Strategy 1. Debriefing

When you conduct a session wrap-up and review, build in some time for a debriefing. Have participants respond to these questions individually or discuss them with a partner and report to the larger group.

- What is the most important thing you learned in today's session?
- What will you remember from this session?
- What did we talk about that you would like to share with your family and friends, co-teacher, or director?
- What's the next step you will take to become "ethically fit"?

Strategy 2. Open-Ended Thoughts

If you have a little more time, you might conduct an informal written evaluation. Asking participants to complete sentences like these that follow will give you good insights into what they gained from your session.

- This discussion of professional ethics has made me more aware of

_____

- I will not forget_____
- The most important thing I learned was _____
- I would like to know more about _____
- I am still confused about_____
- I feel more confident and ethically competent, because now I

_____

These questions can also be built into more formal evaluations such as course evaluations or final reflection papers. In these you can ask students to identify what they learned, how their ethical awareness has been enhanced, and what knowledge and skill they have acquired that will make them more adept at dealing with ethical issues.

Strategy 3. Rating Scale

Another assessment idea is to create a continuum on paper and hang it on the wall. Participants place their initials on the continuum both before and after the session.

I have not heard of NAEYC's Code of Ethical Conduct.	I've heard of or seen the Code somewhere.	I know about the NAEYC Code.	I've read the Code.	I've used the Code of Ethical Conduct in my work.	I teach others about the NAEYC Code.

Or provide an individual continuum for each participant.

I would probably not think of using NAEYC's Code of Ethical Conduct.				The Code influences my work with children and families.

Strategy 4. Reflections

If you are asking participants to devote journal reflections to ethics, you will find the reflection questions in the book *Ethics and the Early Childhood Educator* a useful resource. You may add additional questions to highlight particular concepts or dispositions you want your students or participants to address.

These kinds of questions can lead to fruitful and focused reflections.

- When I am faced with a difficult ethical dilemma in my classroom, I plan to _____

- When I encounter a difficult ethical dilemma in my classroom, I plan to ask _____ to help me weigh my responsibilities, consider the alternatives, and find a defensible resolution.

Observational assessments

Informal, ungraded assessment such as talk-backs and open-ended questions that ask for participants' reflections and impressions don't always provide sufficient evidence of learning. Those who teach preservice teachers or graduate students in college and university settings, for example, have a responsibility to evaluate students' work and translate their judgments into grades.

But measuring students' ethical competence is neither easy nor precise. Of those teacher educators who responded to a survey, 14% reported that they don't make any effort to evaluate students' knowledge or mastery of professional ethics (Freeman & Brown 1996). The reason for this low percentage may be in the difficulty of measuring ethical competence.

Those who did evaluate students' ethical expertise reported that they most often relied on informal techniques such as observations of students' work with young children and their contributions to class discussions. One respondent noted that "Knowing how much students retain in the field is hard to know" (Freeman 1996, 14).

Written assessments

Those who seek an objective approach to evaluating students' knowledge, attitudes, analytical abilities, and dialogical competence with regard to professional ethics may want to design quizzes or tests to address these goals.

Questions targeting basic knowledge of the content of the Code could include

- What is NAEYC, and who is the intended audience for its Code of Ethical Conduct? (This can be structured for a short answer or be designed as a multiple-choice question.)

- Early childhood educators' relationships with what four constituencies are described in the NAEYC Code? (This can be structured for a short answer or as a multiple choice.)
- The Code's first Principle (P-1.1)" has precedence over all others in this Code." What does it require? Restate the Principle in your own words.

   Questions that require analysis and interpretation include

- The Code does not provide answers to every dilemma you are likely to face. How can it be useful to you even in situations it does not specifically address?
- The Code has been called "a living document." What does this tell you about the process of its development and revision?
- What are some of the first things you would do when facing a problem that has no right answer? For example, think about the dilemma created by the mother who asked that her 4-year-old son not nap at school because he couldn't fall asleep at night until well past her own bedtime.
- Give an example of a dilemma with an ethical dimension (see "67 Selected Cases" in Part 4). Ask students or participants to identify the relevant ethical Principle from a group of four or five. Have them describe two or three ethical responses that would address the educator's responsibility or help resolve the dilemma.

And, finally, to assess application and synthesis, the assessment might include questions such as these.

- The Code is useful because it identifies ethical responsibilities and guides practitioners' decisionmaking when they face ethical dilemmas. What is the difference between an *ethical responsibility* and an *ethical dilemma*? Give an example of each.
- Could you work successfully in an early childhood setting with a colleague who knows little about child development or has no desire to learn? With a colleague who has no interest in learning about or observing professional ethical standards? Why or why not?

Ethics assessment in college courses

Instructors may find it useful to integrate subjective questions with the more objective ones given above. Using an essay format, ask students to describe an ethical dilemma based on their personal classroom experiences. This would provide an indication of their abilities to identify the ethical dimensions embedded in the complex realities of the classroom.

Asking students to work through a dilemma they have encountered in their workplace or one described in Part 4, "67 Selected Cases,"can add another layer to assessment. The method of case analysis and a flow chart depicting that process are included in the *Ethics* book (see Chapter 3) and provide a useful model.

Evaluation of case analyses would include a consideration of whether students successfully identify the ethical issues and the stakeholders. Did each apply appropriate sections of the Code to find a defensible resolution? Were the priorities identified and choices made expressed in a clear and convincing manner? This approach, in effect, commits the case discussion process to paper, giving participants/students the opportunity to carefully consider their responses and affording the instructor an opportunity to study learners' work in more detail and depth.

Educators seeking guidance in evaluating their students' analysis of ethical dilemmas may find it helpful to refer to the work of Selma Wasserman and Muriel Bebeau.

Wasserman's work focuses on the process of evaluating students' analysis of realistic cases. She identifies dimensions of (1) intellectual development, (2) skills, and (3) attitudes required for successful case analysis. Using these three major headings, Wasserman creates an instructor's checklist and student's self-evaluation protocol that focus on the quality of the student's thinking, communication of ideas, research skills, personal perspectives, beliefs and values, and self-evaluation (1994, 135–55).

Bebeau addresses the challenges of evaluating instruction in professional ethics, offering a method that measures "ethical sensitivity, moral judgment, moral motivation and commitment and moral implementation abilities, and learning experiences to promote their attainment" (1993, 316). Her method includes techniques to evaluate students' oral responses to videotaped scenarios, checklists to analyze written responses to ethical dilemmas, several protocols to evaluate moral motivation and commitment, and checklists to evaluate application skills during simulations. She offers these materials as models (patterned after those developed by dental educators), which she believes hold promise for those who work with preservice and inservice teachers.

The fact is that helping students translate theory into practice is the real objective of ethics instruction. But evaluating the success of these efforts is a difficult task. Documenting appropriate uses of the Code in the unpredictable, highly charged, and sensitive circumstances of real-life practice is much more difficult than assessing students' knowledge of the Code in a course or workshop.

We cannot count on seeing evidence of students' ability to apply the Code during our routine visits to observe them in classrooms, nor can we rely on written exams to capture the dimensions of the knowledge, judgment, and decisionmaking that are involved when they actually base their work on the Code. These are undoubtedly some of the reasons that so many early childhood teacher educators report they rely on their observations and instincts rather than on formal assessment tools to evaluate students' ethical expertise.

Self-assessment and professional portfolios

Working professionals may wish or need to assess their developing knowledge and skill in professional ethics. For adult learners who are setting their own learning goals, assessment should be designed to help them to gauge and document their professional competence. Additionally, as compensation and career status become more tied to professional development, practitioners may be required to provide proof of their learning to retain a credential or advance in their careers.

How can a practitioner assess and document her or his ethical fitness in the real world? A test, whether addressing basic knowledge or analytical and problem-solving skill, only evaluates theoretical knowledge. An alternative strategy is the professional portfolio.

You can help practitioners verify their ethical knowledge and skill in the following ways:

- **Document training.** Provide a single-page description of the workshop, workshop series, or course, including the title, content, and level of the training; sponsor of the training; the date and duration of the training; and your name, title, and qualifications.

- **Document learning.** Use one of the methods (Strategies 1, 2, 3, or 4) described earlier in this section to provide some tangible evidence of participants' learning.

- **Document knowledge application.** Provide participants with an easy-to-use format (see the sample "Training Documentation and Action Plan" on p. 72) for planning ways to implement their acquired learning and to document their competence.

- **Document competence.** Encourage participants to use written self-reflections in the form of a journal or diary as a tool to document the ways in which they address the ongoing ethical responsibilities and dilemmas they encounter. Selected entries (with the names protected of specific children, families, colleagues, and programs) can then be used as part of a portfolio to demonstrate participants' ethical fitness in the real world.

Training Documentation and Action Plan

Course or workshop title _____

Date(s), number of sessions, and duration of training _____

Training sponsor_____

Presenter's name and qualifications_____

Level of training: Beginning, midlevel, advanced _____

Description of the training _____

_____

_____

[e.g., A two-hour workshop designed to acquaint participants with the NAEYC Code of Ethical Conduct. Participants will be given an overview of the Code, opportunities to interact with the Code, and practice using the Code to identify ethical responsibilities and to select ethical responses to dilemmas.]

Participant's Plan of Action

As a result of what I have learned in this training, I plan to integrate the following action(s) into my practice:

I plan to document my action(s) in the following ways:

Evaluating teaching

Even though we may not know if participants in our conference sessions, inservice workshops, or classes will put what we teach into practice, we can and should evaluate the effectiveness of our presentations. This process begins with candid reflection and self-evaluation.

First, we can think about our preparation. Did we prepare thoroughly, study our notes, and preview our delivery before we began? How well did we capture the audience's attention? For example, did the newspaper headlines, comics, or personal examples elicit smiles of recognition and nods of agreement? Did our questions effectively launch lively conversations? Did participants raise challenging questions that showed they understood and were thinking about the information we presented?

Feeney, Freeman, and Moravcik

In addition to reflecting on our effectiveness, we can ask participants for specific feedback about our presentations. We can ask them if the activities and discussion questions we used helped them understand and be ready to apply the Code to their work with young children. These questions could be added as part of a talk-back or written evaluation we ask participants to complete at the end of our session, workshop, or course unit on ethics.

The following kinds of questions are likely to get to the heart of the matter and help you continually refine the session, workshop, or course work you have created that focuses on ethics:

- What will you remember about this session?
- Did the games we engaged in help you learn more about the NAEYC Code and its application? If so, how?
- What aspects of this session were most meaningful or helpful to you?
- Is there any part of this session you think we should eliminate or change in the future?
- Would you recommend that a friend attend this session/class/workshop? Why or why not?

Conclusion

We know that learning ethics is never finished, for ethical decisionmaking is a one-on-one, case-by-case process. Ethical behavior requires careful thought and reflection, pride and humility, a willingness to change, and the courage to remain steadfast. Karl D. Hostetler observes that "Ethics need not, and probably should not, always be at the forefront of teachers' minds. But it persists as a background project, as teachers are continually searching for . . . what is ethically right and good" (Hostetler & Hostetler 1997, 196).

We hope you find the resources in this book helpful in preparing for and gauging your success toward achieving the goal of equipping early childhood educators with the knowledge, skills, and dispositions they need to apply the NAEYC Code effectively as they work with young children and their families.

IV
Teaching Resources

Sixty-Seven Selected Cases

We have collected cases related to ethical issues in early care and education since we began to work on the development of the NAEYC Code of Ethical Conduct. Some cases that follow were submitted in response to the first ethics survey in *Young Children* (Feeney & Kipnis 1985). Others are contributions to the ongoing series "Using the NAEYC Code of Ethics" in *Young Children.* Some are adaptations from cases in *Getting Ethical: A Resource Book for Workshop Leaders* (Fasoli & Woodrow 1991) and *Will My Response Be Ethical? A Reflective Process to Guide the Practice of Early Childhood Students and Professionals* (Newman & Pollnitz 1999). And still others are based on ethical issues experienced in our work or shared with us by early childhood educators as we explored professional ethics over the years.

When you use cases in your courses or workshops, it's important to select those reflecting the issues most relevant for your group or containing content you particularly want to highlight. You might embellish the cases by adding names of fictitious centers, schools, and individuals to reflect the identity of your community.

Most of the cases given in the next few pages involve identifying and balancing two or more responsibilities—some (marked with an **R**) require careful attention to a specific responsibility. Cases have been organized by sections of the NAEYC Code and within each section by the type of issue addressed. They are numbered to indicate the section of the Code and the number of the case within that section (case 2.11. refers to the 11th case relating to "Section 2: Ethical responsibilities to families"). Cases that are analyzed in depth in *Ethics and the Early Childhood Educator* are identified in brackets at the end of the case. Cases are printed in a format that allows them to be duplicated and made into cards.

Ethical responsibilities to children: Code Section 1

A relatively small percentage of the dilemmas faced by early childhood educators, as Chapter 1 of *Ethics and the Early Childhood Educator* notes, fit into this category. Most often, situations that focus on children involve their welfare or require early childhood educators to balance the needs of an individual child against their responsibilities to the entire group.

- Individual needs versus group needs: Case Cards 1.1 and 1.2.
- Child abuse: Case Cards 1.3 through 1.7.
- Equitable treatment: Case Cards 1.8 and 1.9.

Ethical responsibilities to families: Code Section 2

The ethical issues most frequently reported by early childhood educators concern relationships with families. Most of the situations involve obligations that are in conflict. Other issues have to do with divorce and custody, confidentiality, and situations in which families and early childhood educators have different ideas about what children should be learning.

- Conflicting obligations (complex client cases): Case Cards 2.1 through 2.7.
- Divorce and custody: Case Cards 2.8 through 2.12.
- Information management: Case Cards 2.13 through 2.18.

Ethical responsibilities to colleagues: Code Section 3

Ethical issues involving colleagues are also frequently reported by early childhood educators. These involve information management, professional behavior, and program practices.

- Information management: Case Cards 3.1 through 3.14.
- Professional behavior: Case Cards 3.15 through 3.17.
- Child abuse: Case Cards 3.18 through 3.21.
- Program practice: Case Cards 3.22 through 3.28.
- Administration/personnel policies: Case Cards 3.29 through 3.32.

Ethical responsibilities to community and society: Code Section 4

Teachers' concerns about suspected child abuse fit into this category, as do violations of regulations designed to protect children and situations that call on early childhood educators to care for and about the welfare of all children.

- Child abuse/neglect: Case Cards 4.1 and 4.2.
- Laws and regulations: Case Cards 4.3 through 4.8.

Feeney, Freeman, and Moravcik

1.1 A large and extremely aggressive 4-year-old boy in your class is frightening and hurting other children. Your director and a mental health specialist have been unable to help. His parents feel that his behavior is typical for boys his age; they won't get counseling. You and your co-teacher are becoming stressed and tired, and you are worried that the other children are not getting the attention they need.
[*Ethics*, Case 1]

1.2 One 3-year-old in your class spends most of her time rolling a truck alongside the block area. She howls and disrupts large-group activities and bangs her head to put herself to sleep at naptime. Her pediatrician has told her parents, "She will grow out of it." You've found she needs constant one-on-one attention, and other children's parents are beginning to complain that this child takes too much of the adults' time and energy.
[*Ethics*, Case 2]

1.3 A 5-year-old in your class is showing the classic signs of abuse: multiple bruises, frequent black eyes, and psychological withdrawal. Her mother, a high-strung woman, says her child falls a lot, but you have not observed that the girl is clumsy. Twice the child's father seemed to be drunk when he picked her up at school.
[*Ethics*, Case 10]

R

1.4 You are a teacher in a preschool. A mother often tells you how proud she is of her daughter, although you have heard her speaking harshly to the child. One day the child comes to school visibly upset and tells you that her mother spanked her in the middle of the night. You ask the mother about it, and she explains that she spanked her child because she wet the bed. When you tell the mom that bed-wetting is a not-unusual occurrence that usually disappears in time, she tells you that spanking cured her older daughter of bed-wetting.

Note: Cases referred to by numbers in brackets beneath the case description appear in *Ethics and the Early Childhood Educator*.

1.5 You are a kindergarten teacher. One student's mother comes to pick up her child and drive him home. From her slurred speech and clumsy movements, you suspect that she has been drinking heavily after work. Variation on 1.5: The mother arrives by bus and plans to take the child home on the bus.

1.6 You have successfully taught first grade in a predominantly Hispanic neighborhood for several years, and your efforts to understand the culture are appreciated. One day a father with whom you have a particularly good relationship remarks in a parent meeting that he regularly swats his child with a belt to keep him in line and teach him respect. Soon after hearing this remark, you see marks on the child's back and legs that could have been left by a belt. You realize there are cultural differences about appropriate discipline for young children and are troubled by what appears to be abuse.
[*Ethics*, Variation 2 on Case 10]   **R**

1.7 You work in a preschool that serves several families who are recent immigrants from a Muslim country. After the winter holidays, a 4-year-old girl in your class has difficulty walking and refuses to go to the bathroom. You take her to the toilet and see that she is healing from female circumcision, a custom that is accepted and common in her family's country of origin.

R

1.8 You are the director of a prestigious preschool with a long waiting list. You are fortunate because a wealthy benefactor donates lots of money to your school each year. The chairman of the board of your program comes to you and explains that the wealthy benefactor's daughter is moving back to the community with her 2-year-old son. The chairman asks you to enroll the benefactor's grandson immediately.

1.9 You are a family child care provider. You have accepted a child with HIV / AIDS in your program because you know that the disease has never been transmitted in a preschool setting (Freeman 2000), and you feel this family deserves a chance. Although you have respected the family's confidentiality, as required by law, somehow the other families find out and threaten to withdraw their children from your care.

2.1 The mother of a 4-year-old in your class has asked that he not nap at school, because when he naps he stays up too late at night, making it difficult for her to get up at 5 a.m. to go to work. He seems to need his nap to stay in good spirits in the afternoon.
[*Ethics*, Case 3]

2.2 You are a preschool director who notices that a child in the 3-year-old group falls asleep every morning just before her group goes outdoors. In conversations with the mother, you learn that the child is kept up late at night because her father doesn't come home from work until 9:00 p.m. While you appreciate that it is important for the child to spend time with her father, you do not have enough staff to assign a teacher to stay inside with her during her morning nap.

Feeney, Freeman, and Moravcik

2.3 A parent calls you, the center director, to express concern that her 3-year-old daughter is permitted to walk the short distance to the bathroom without an adult accompanying her and waiting. You reassure her that the security in your center is good, but she insists that her child must be individually escorted to the bathroom.

2.4 A father informs you, the center director, that his daughter, who has chronic asthma, needs to stay indoors every time he suspects the child is becoming ill. At first you try to accommodate him, but with growing enrollment this becomes impossible. The staffing problem has been explained to the parent, but he feels that the school should be able to provide service to children like his who have chronic health problems.

2.5 Your center serves snack and lunch. One child is always asking for food, and the child's parent feels the child should always get food when she expresses a desire for it. The parent says that you are abusing the child when you do not provide food whenever she wants it.

2.6 You are a new graduate who has accepted a position teaching kindergarten at a rural school in a low-income area where students' test scores are very low. You have set up learning centers, and things are going well. You are shocked when your principal tells you the students' parents are adamant that they don't want children to "just play." They expect children to bring home workbook pages they have completed in school and expect that kind of homework too.
[*Ethics*, Case 4]

2.7 A father comes to see you, complaining that his 4-year-old son has been allowed to wear a dress in school. He is furious and tells you that you are supposed to be teaching the child to read and write not to dress up like a girl.

2.8 You are the teacher of a 7-year-old whose parents are going through a very contentious divorce. You have been asked by the child's mother to testify on her behalf at the child custody hearing.

2.9 The custodial parent of a 2-year-old in the preschool you direct requests that the school provide no information to the noncustodial parent (although you have not been informed of a restraining order limiting the noncustodial parent's access to the child). The noncustodial parent, who visits the child occasionally at the school and picks up the child on a regular basis for visitation, requests a parent conference to keep informed about the child's progress.

R

2.10 You are the teacher of a 4-year-old whose parents were divorced last year, with joint custody granted. At school the child's provocative and hostile behavior suggests the stress she is experiencing following the divorce and her father's remarriage. The director has requested that both parents attend a conference to discuss the child's behavior, but the mother refuses to meet with the father and his new wife. Both mother and father would like sole custody.

2.11 The father and custodial parent of a 4-year-old in the program you direct has changed since his divorce. He always looks stressed and avoids contact with the staff. He neglects to sign the child out of school each day, a violation of school policy, and has twice caused minor damage with his car in the parking lot. The child is now absent two or three days per week and is usually late for school when she does come. The father became very angry with the staff and his daughter when her lunch box was misplaced. Efforts to talk with him have been unsuccessful. The girl's mother (and the noncustodial parent), visits her often at the school during the day and seems genuinely concerned about her welfare. She asks how it is going with the father.

2.12 You are a preschool director. The mother of a girl who is new in your class is very nervous. She explains to you that her child is *never* to go on field trips and *never* to have her picture taken. She and her daughter are very loving to one another. One day, when the child is absent, a man arrives at the school and explains that the child is his daughter and his wife has kidnapped her. He shows you custody papers and an article from an out-of-state newspaper that describes the kidnapping and has a picture of the child. He asks you to give him the mother's address and phone number or call to notify him just as soon as the child returns to school.

2.13 You are a teacher of a second-grade class that includes several children with special needs. You are uncomfortable when parents ask questions about children in your class, and you don't know how to respond when they ask, "What's wrong with him," "Why does he behave like that?" or "How do you handle her slowness?"

R

2.14 One morning a parent approaches you, the head teacher, and starts to chat. After a while she says, "I just can't understand how Mrs._____ could have both of her children in the 3-year-olds group. Is it true that her children are only three months apart in age?" Fortunately an episode of sand throwing requires your quick intervention, enabling you to avoid responding to the question. But the next morning, she repeats the question.

R

2.15 A parent of a child in your kindergarten class has told you that the family follows a strict vegetarian regimen for spiritual as well as health reasons. This parent tells you her son has had no interest in meat or fish and he should not be encouraged to eat these foods. The child soon becomes quite interested in other children's lunches. One day you find the child taking a bite from his friend's ham sandwich. The child begs you not to tell his parents because he would be punished. He says he didn't like the ham and was sorry he had tried it. You think no harm has been done and don't tell the family about the incident. Two weeks later you see the child and his buddy quietly swap sandwiches—cheese for chicken!

2.16 A 2-year-old in your group often bites other children when he is angry or excited. You have talked to the parents about this behavior and are concerned to learn of the harsh discipline they use with the child. The day after the child has bitten a classmate during some rough-and-tumble play, his mother brings him to school and asks you how he has been behaving lately. She reminds you that if he gets into any trouble, she and her husband want to know so they can deal with it.

2.17 A classmate bites a 20-month-old boy in your group in an altercation over a toy. You apply ice and comfort him and write a report of the incident for the school files. When the mother picks him up, she is informed that her son was bitten during play, that the skin was not broken, and that ice was applied. The mother is angry about what happened. "Who bit him?" she demands.

R

2.18 You are a family child care provider. A parent of a child in your care confides in you and tells you that she is having marital difficulties. Your best friend, another parent, suspects that this family is having problems. She pumps you for information.

R

3.1 You and your assistant are working in the staff room after school with several colleagues from other classrooms. This morning you both had been informed that the father of one of your students had moved out of the house the previous evening. One of the other teachers notes that she observed that this child had been very aggressive all day. Your assistant remarks, "It's not surprising, you won't believe what his father did this time. His mother told us this morning." She then proceeds to relate the entire story of the break up. [*Ethics*, Case 6]

3.2 You are a teacher in a child care center with a large staff. You hear some staff members talking negatively about colleagues who are not present. You feel uncomfortable listening, and you are becoming increasingly concerned because this kind of talk occurs frequently. The director is always busy and is only willing to discuss issues that involve children.

3.3 You are a preschool director. One day you go to a classroom to give a teacher a message at naptime and observe two teachers discussing the home life of a child whose father has been arrested for drunk driving.

3.4 Your co-teacher is often angry at administrative decisions made in the center. On a number of occasions you have heard her complaining about these things to parents.

3.5 You have a child in your room who has been diagnosed as having attention deficit hyperactivity disorder (ADHD). He sometimes scares the younger children with his boisterous and frenetic activity. A parent who is a kindergarten teacher notices his behavior and asks you what the problem is.

3.6 A 4-year-old in your group who is usually happy and cooperative has been irritable. He plays by himself, seldom smiles or laughs, and frequently quarrels with the other children. You mention the change in his behavior to his mother. She tells you that she and her husband have been arguing a great deal and have decided to get a divorce. So far they have told no one. A few days later, you are working with a volunteer when the child spills paint on the floor. She asks the child to help her clean it up, but he refuses. She asks him a second time, gently but firmly, and he shouts that he will not. He starts screaming and knocks over two cans of paint. It takes half an hour to calm him. Later you and the volunteer sit down for coffee, and she is still upset at the child's behavior.

3.7 You are the assistant director at a preschool, and you are asked by your beautician about a teacher at your school. You ask her why she is inquiring. She tells you that when another teacher from your school was having her hair cut the other day, she said that this teacher can't control the rowdy boys in her class.

3.8 You are a preschool director and schedule a conference with a mental health consultant for your teachers to discuss the progress of a child having behavioral problems. At the meeting, while the child's progress is being reviewed and treatment goals are being revised, you become concerned that the teachers are volunteering detailed information about the child's family.

3.9 You are a preschool teacher. On one occasion you find yourself seated next to a pediatrician who is a well-known expert on child abuse. You realize that this presents a great opportunity, and you ask for information that might help you decide what to do about a child in your group whom you suspect is being physically abused. The doctor gives you some general advice but says that he needs to know more about the situation to give you better guidance.

3.10 You recently went out to dinner with a group of friends and acquaintances, including a therapist who works with young children who are emotionally disturbed. During dinner the therapist asks you about the behavior of a child in your class. She says that the child's mother has asked her to visit your classroom to observe her daughter's behavior with other children, and naturally she was interested in your opinion.

3.11 You are a teacher in a Christian preschool and also a member of the sponsoring church. All preschool employees are required to sign a contract agreeing to follow high standards of moral behavior. You like and respect the teacher who works in the classroom next to yours, and the two of you sometimes talk about your private lives. She is a single parent. One day she tells you that she works as a topless dancer in a nightclub to help support her child. She asks you not to tell the director or the board, who would fire her for breach of contract.

3.12 You are a preschool director who hears through the grapevine that a former employee of yours was charged with abusing her own child but was acquitted. You receive a call from another director who says that the former employee has given your name as a reference and she is considering hiring her.

3.13 You have been informed that a 2-year-old in the next classroom has been diagnosed with contagious diarrhea. You expect that the families will be alerted to the illness through a posted notice, but the director of your center has dismissed the problem. She tells teachers to be sure to wear gloves and wash their hands after changing the child. You go to the director and express your concern. The director says she doesn't want to upset the parents and that good hygiene should take care of the problem.

R

3.14 Everyone in your school goes on an outing to the zoo. When you return to school you find, huddled up and terrified, a 3-year-old who was left behind in school. The director decides not to report the incident to the parents. Staff members have been warned not to discuss the episode at all.

R

3.15 You and your co-teacher work with a group of twenty 4-year-olds (two of whom have special needs) in an inner-city child development center. Your classroom is a portable building, one of six units clustered around a small, central courtyard. Several times recently your co-teacher has left the classroom for periods of up to 30 minutes to conduct personal business.
[*Ethics*, Case 5]

3.16 You teach in a community preschool. One afternoon in the lounge you hear a co-worker make an insulting joke about children and families of a particular ethnic group. It makes you feel uncomfortable, and you think her comments show an unhealthy prejudice; however, everyone else laughs.

3.17 You are a preschool teacher. The teacher in the class next door is not doing a great job. She often comes in without any plans made and borrows activities from you. Her classroom is chaotic, and you have seen children doing things you think are inappropriate, even dangerous.

3.18 The teacher in the next room has always been brusque with the children. Lately, however, you are becoming increasingly concerned about her open hostility and harshness toward children. You have seen her shake a child and heard her belittle a child.

3.19 You teach in a public school kindergarten. You are on good terms with the other teachers but feel they do not completely accept you because you are young and enthusiastic about teaching. The first-grade teacher in the classroom next to yours has the reputation of being a strict disciplinarian. You go into her room one day to borrow some paper, and you see her hit a child.

R

3.20 A 6-year-old boy in your class began to cry when it was time for him to go to the resource teacher. He complained that she scared him and thumped him on the head. You approach her later and tell her of the child's comment. She denies the accusation, saying that he was lying. Since you know she was removed from a regular classroom because of complaints that she was shaking and hitting children, you believe that the child was telling the truth.

R

3.21 You teach in a school that has a population from a culture in which physical punishment is common. One morning you observe a boy from this cultural group strike another child. A new aide who shares this culture grabs him and twists his ear. The child was momentarily stunned but soon seemed fine and was calm for the rest of the day. Apart from some redness, there were no other effects. When you speak with the aide, she tells you that children in her community are used to this discipline. She says, "It calmed him down, didn't it?"

3.22 You are an assistant teacher in a class of 3-year-olds. One of your students becomes very aggressive when his mother leaves him each morning. The lead teacher makes him sit on a stool when he begins to get out of control. You feel that discipline should be constructive and reflect an understanding of what has triggered the misbehavior. You want to let the child pound clay or find another safe outlet for his energy.
[*Ethics*, Case 7]

3.23 You are an assistant teacher in a class of 4-year-olds. You are quite concerned about some of the routines the teacher insists on following. She requires children to put away all the art supplies before moving on to the next learning center. The next child to do the activity has to take all the supplies out again. You feel that the teacher takes general principles, such as having children be responsible for cleaning up their own work, and applies these rigidly to all situations, never stopping to ask if the children are benefiting.

3.24 You have just graduated from an early childhood education program. You understand about developmentally appropriate practice and the value of play. You take a job working in a child care center near your home and are delighted that it pays well. You are surprised to find that you are expected to have your 3- and 4-year-olds sit for long hours each day and do worksheets. When you question this approach, you are told that this is how they have always taught and teachers and families are very happy with it.
[*Ethics*, Case 8]

3.25 Other teachers in your center have their classes celebrate Mickey Mouse's birthday, watch cartoon videos, dance to rap music, and paint with chocolate pudding. You think that these activities are pointless and do not support children's development. Your colleagues maintain that the children and adults are having fun, and that's justification enough. You believe that any planned activity must have a developmental purpose, be meaningful to children, and be age appropriate.
[*Ethics*, Variation on Case 8]

3.26 You are the director of a church-sponsored preschool and learn from an assistant teacher that the teacher in her group has presented to her 3- and 4-year-olds the Easter story, complete with graphic details about the suffering and death of Jesus. The assistant registers a strong objection to this curriculum. She is worried that the children will be frightened by the story. You agree with her concerns.

3.27 You are an experienced teacher with a degree in early childhood education. Your 4-year-old daughter attends the school where you teach. She has been placed in the class of a new teacher who used to teach in an elementary school. You are concerned about the worksheets she is bringing home each day. You go to the director to register your objection, both as a parent and as a staff member. You see a workbook that your daughter's teacher has left in the office—it is meant for grade two! The director sympathizes with your concern and tells you she will discuss it with the teacher next week. Three weeks later the flow of worksheets continues.

3.28 You are a kindergarten teacher in an inner-city elementary school. All the children in your school are required to take the Metropolitan Readiness Test during the first week of kindergarten. The three-day test is administered solely to determine qualifications for federal funding. You think that it is an ordeal for the children that is both frustrating and demeaning. You protest, but the administration insists that you give the children the test.

3.29 You are a preschool teacher. Finally, after two frustrating years of not having a good assistant teacher, you have a great one. She's reliable, has training, is smart, and is great with kids. Your director comes to you and explains that she has an opening for a teacher in another class. She asks if you think your assistant might be a good person for the job.

3.30 You are the director at a children's center where there is a teacher's job open. A former colleague from another program applies for the position. She is the most qualified candidate and a great teacher, but you never liked her personally.

3.31 You are a center director and have been approached by the corporation that runs your program and asked to use a highly academic curriculum that takes up most of each morning. This makes you very uncomfortable. Your continued good relationship with your employer and possibly your job are dependent on your agreeing to this request.

3.32 You are the director of a child care center. The church in which your program is housed has decided to sponsor adult day care for the elderly. To make room for it, you will have to close a classroom, reduce enrollment and lay off staff. You have two choices. You can lay off "Grandma," who is loved by the parents and has been with the center for many years. Grandma is only minimally competent by today's standards and has no training or credentials. Your other choice is to lay off the teacher who was hired most recently. She is young and well trained and does a good job in the classroom.

4.1 You are the director of a child care center. A child in your center shows definite signs of being abused. You know that you should report the case to your local child protective services agency. But the last time you referred a child to them, a worker visited the family but did not promptly intervene. The family left town, never to be heard from again.

R

4.2 A child in your class has been abandoned by his mother and is cared for by an uncle and his girlfriend, whom you suspect are drug dealers. You document numerous instances of neglect and emotional abuse, which you report to your local child protective services agency. An investigation is made, and the child is allowed to remain in the uncle's home. The situation does not appear to be improving.

R

4.3 When you accepted your job of caring for infants, you were not informed about state child care regulations. After several months you learned that your state requires a ratio no greater than 1:4 for children younger than 12 months old. You were teaching alone in a group that sometimes had as many as seven children in it. When the licensing worker came to inspect, the director sent the cook to your classroom and told the worker that she works regularly in your classroom.
[*Ethics*, Case 9]

R

4.4 You are a preschool teacher who has just moved to another state and taken a job. You have always included lots of cooking in your curriculum and believe that it is a great way to motivate children and integrate learning. After your first cooking project, the director of your new school takes you aside and tells you that cooking is against licensing rules in this state because of potential health and safety risks to children.

4.5 A number of families have recently moved their children to your center from another one in your neighborhood. They have told you stories of what happened to their children in that center. They describe "dirty sheets on the cots," "placing children in the sun to sleep when they're naughty," "withholding food as punishment," and "twenty children to one adult." One day on your way to work, you drive by to check it out for yourself. You see a lot covered with asphalt and dry grass. There are a few rusting pieces of playground equipment. Several children are looking through a chainlink fence. There are no adults in sight.

4.6 You are a family child care provider. You receive funding from the government for your food program. The food program rules say that you cannot serve the children leftovers from the previous meal. Sometimes that means you have to throw away perfectly good food.

4.7 You are a center director. The teachers in your school have high heels for children to wear in the dress-up corner. The children enjoy them, and they seem to encourage elaborate make-believe play. Recently your new licensing worker has been telling directors that they must get rid of high heels because these could be used by children as weapons. You learn that this inspector will be coming to your school next week for your annual inspection.

4.8 You are the director of a preschool that serves families with low incomes. Your rent is very low, which allows you to charge a low tuition to families. Your landlord has let the building fall into dangerous disrepair. There are no other low-rent facilities that could house a preschool in your community.

Value Choices

The choices we make in what we value are personal. The 36 reproducible signs that follow are one collection, which could be expanded to reflect even greater diversity (and variety culturally, geographically, and experientially) or enlarged to include ideas from a list that students brainstorm.

The signs serve as a tool for "Activity 4. Values Auction" (p. 21) in Part 2. It is useful to reproduce the signs in a large enough quantity (duplicates and triplicates are OK) to ensure active and comparative bidding during the activity.

the arts	adventure
the arts	**adventure**
charity	**beauty**
comfort	**children**

competence	community
diversity	**creativity**
fairness	**education**

family	faith
friendship	freedom
health	happiness

heritage & culture

humor

individuality

helping others

honesty & integrity

independence

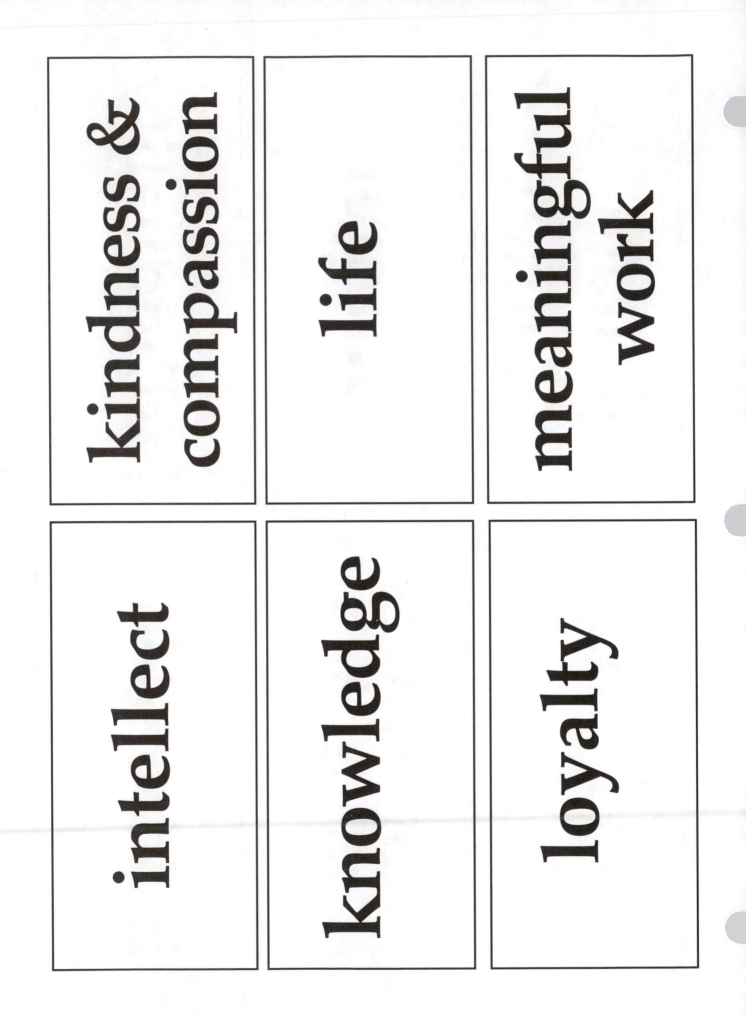

kindness & compassion

life

meaningful work

intellect

knowledge

loyalty

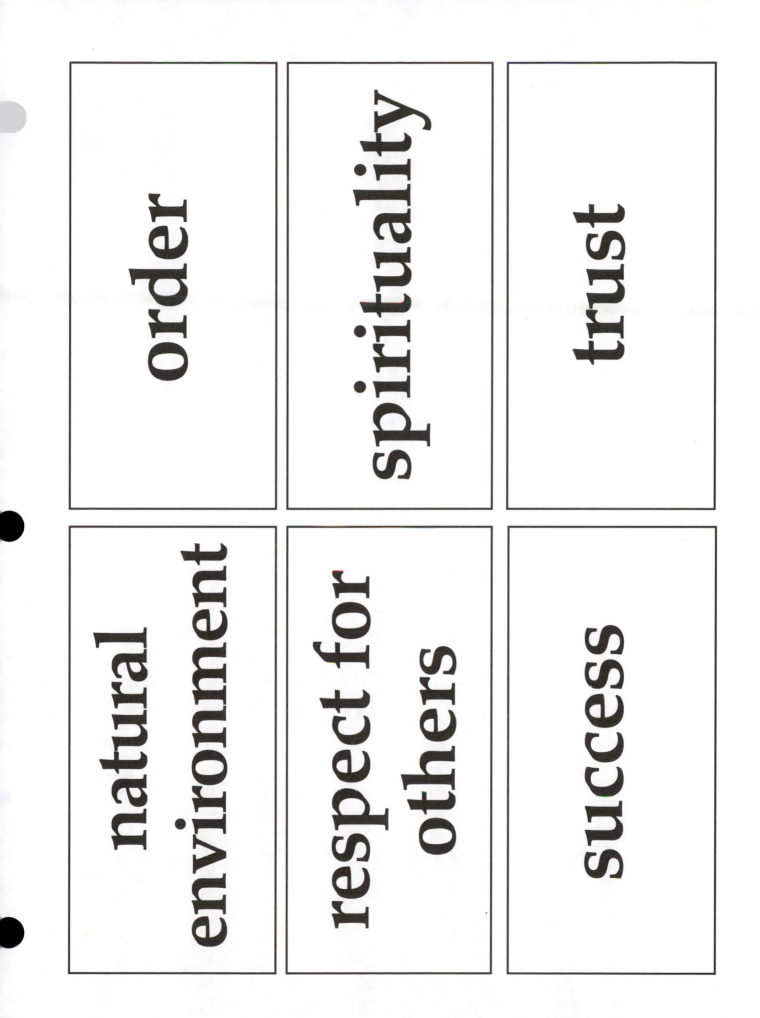

order

spirituality

trust

natural environment

respect for others

success

Is It Ethical? Game

T his game was created to provide a safe, nonthreatening method for students or workshop participants to consider the issues involved in a situation, weigh another's response, and then decide if they think the response is ethical or not ethical. It lets participants react and interact in a game dynamic that is stimulating and challenging. It provides an opportunity to use the NAEYC Code of Ethical Conduct and gives firsthand experience of how the Code is useful in addressing ethical choices.

Preparation and directions for playing

Situation card sets A and B represent dilemmas early childhood practitioners and administrators face in their work with children and families. The situations are drawn from the 67 cases presented in the first section of this Part 4. Set A has 16 situations and a practitioner focus; Set B has 8 situations and an administrator focus. Sets A and B have master sheets that provide a scoring code and references to the specific Principles or Ideals in the NAEYC Code of Ethical Conduct on which answers are based. The teacher/trainer duplicates the situation cards and master sheets that follow to provide the number of sets needed for a class or workshop.

Form small groups of three to six players. Have each group select a dealer (group leader). Explain that the cards describe situations that pose dilemmas for early childhood educators, and in each case the issue is stated and a response given. Preset the time limit for play.

The object of the game

The object of the game is to have players consider and use the Code. Players take turns reading situation cards aloud to their group. Each player rates the response to the situation as **ethical** or **not ethical.** Players then use the Code to justify their responses. Later they have the opportunity to compare their responses to the master sheets.

Materials needed

Each small group receives a deck of situation cards (sets A or B or both) and a copy of the *NAEYC Code of Ethical Conduct and Statement of Commitment*. Provide tally sheets or ask participants to use a blank sheet of paper. Give the master sheets to the dealer in each group.

Steps in playing

1. The dealer shuffles the situation cards and deals them face down to the players until all cards are dealt.

2. In turn, beginning to the dealer's right, each player selects one of his or her cards, indicates its number, and reads aloud to the group the situation, the issue, and the response made.

3. The other players silently decide whether the response is ethical or not ethical. Each player writes **E** if it is ethical or **NE** if it is not ethical next to the situation number on the tally sheet or blank paper without showing his or her answer.

4. When all players have recorded their answers to a situation, each in turn tells the group what she or he decided and why.

5. All players then look in the NAEYC Code for one or more Principle(s) or Ideal(s) that suggest what the ethical response is in the given situation.

6. Players share with the group what they found and write the numbers of the Principles or Ideals in the NAEYC Code that they think are relevant next to their vote on the tally sheet.

7. Play continues, moving around the game table to each player and hearing as many situations as possible until the dealer calls the preset time limit.

Scoring

Scoring in this game is *optional*. The real purpose is to get participants to use the Code. If scoring is desired, while the dealer shares the ethical/not ethical answers and Principles/Ideals from the master sheet(s), players check their individual tally sheets. Each player may then receive one point if she or he agreed with the master list when voting **E** or **NE** and a second point if she or he found one or more of the matching Principles or Ideals from the list.

Determining a winner(s)

It is important for the teacher/trainer to emphasize the point that everyone who plays the game is a winner, because every player benefits if he or she used the Code and made connections between his or her ethical choices and the Code's Principles and Ideals. The only way to lose is to fail to use the Code to help determine ethical responses. If you decide to score the game, add up points (see scoring), then congratulate the high scorers as well as everyone else.

The Broken Marriage

You are a family child care provider. A parent of a child in your care confides in you and tells you that she is having marital difficulties. Your best friend, another parent, suspects that this family is having problems. She pumps you for information.

The issue: Do you reveal anything? Do you risk your friendship by refusing OR share the information and swear your friend to secrecy?

Response: You share a little bit! In this community you know that word is going to get around sooner or later; it isn't worth jeopardizing your friendship.

IS IT ETHICAL? • 1A

The Bed Wetter

You are a teacher in a preschool. A mother often tells you how proud she is of her daughter, although you have heard her speaking harshly to the child. One day the child comes to school visibly upset and tells you that her mother spanked her in the middle of the night. You ask the mother about it, and she explains that she spanked her child because she wet the bed. When you tell the mom that bed-wetting is a not-unusual occurrence that usually disappears in time, she tells you that spanking cured her older daughter of bed-wetting.

The issue: Do you call children's protective services and report the parent OR allow the parent to continue to spank her child for something out of the child's control?

Response: You don't report. You don't want to cause family stress.

IS IT ETHICAL? • 2A

The Great Assistant

You are a preschool teacher. Finally, after two frustrating years of not having a good assistant teacher, you have a great one. She's reliable, has training, is smart, and is great with kids. Your director comes to you and explains that she has an opening for a teacher in another class. She asks if you think your assistant might be a good person for the job.

The issue: Do you tell her yes and go back to having lousy help OR say yes and know the children's education will be jeopardized? (You know she would do a great job.)

Response: You say, "No, I don't really think she's ready," hoping that the director will find someone else.

IS IT ETHICAL? • 3A

The Aggressive Child

You are a preschool teacher. A large and extremely aggressive 4-year-old boy in your class is frightening and hurting other children. Your director and a mental health specialist have been unable to help. His parents feel that his behavior is typical for boys his age; they won't get counseling. You and your co-teacher are becoming stressed and tired, and you are worried that the other children are not getting the attention they need.

The issue: Do you ask the director to remove the child from your class OR do you decide to keep on trying even though other children are suffering from lack of attention?

Response: You tell the director you cannot keep on working with this child and that you will leave if the child is not removed.

IS IT ETHICAL? • 4A

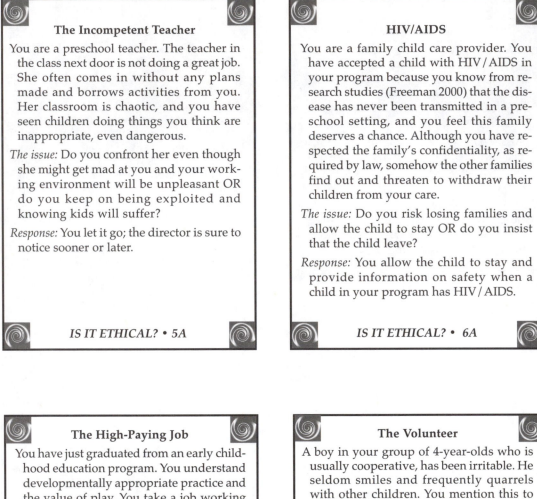

The Incompetent Teacher

You are a preschool teacher. The teacher in the class next door is not doing a great job. She often comes in without any plans made and borrows activities from you. Her classroom is chaotic, and you have seen children doing things you think are inappropriate, even dangerous.

The issue: Do you confront her even though she might get mad at you and your working environment will be unpleasant OR do you keep on being exploited and knowing kids will suffer?

Response: You let it go; the director is sure to notice sooner or later.

IS IT ETHICAL? • 5A

HIV/AIDS

You are a family child care provider. You have accepted a child with HIV/AIDS in your program because you know from research studies (Freeman 2000) that the disease has never been transmitted in a preschool setting, and you feel this family deserves a chance. Although you have respected the family's confidentiality, as required by law, somehow the other families find out and threaten to withdraw their children from your care.

The issue: Do you risk losing families and allow the child to stay OR do you insist that the child leave?

Response: You allow the child to stay and provide information on safety when a child in your program has HIV/AIDS.

IS IT ETHICAL? • 6A

The High-Paying Job

You have just graduated from an early childhood education program. You understand developmentally appropriate practice and the value of play. You take a job working in a child care center near your home and are delighted that it pays well. You are surprised to find that you are expected to have your 3- and 4-year-olds sit for long hours each day and do worksheets. When you question this approach, you are told, "This is how we have always taught, and the teachers and families are very happy with it."

The issue: Do you keep working at a good paying job with a program that isn't good for children OR quit and take a less well-paid job?

Response: You keep the job. Maybe you can change things.

IS IT ETHICAL? • 7A

The Volunteer

A boy in your group of 4-year-olds who is usually cooperative, has been irritable. He seldom smiles and frequently quarrels with other children. You mention this to his mother. She tells you she and her husband have been arguing and have decided to divorce. A few days later when you are working with a volunteer, the child spills paint. She asks the child to help clean it up, but he refuses. She asks him a second time, and he shouts that he will not. He starts screaming and knocks over more paint. During naptime, you and the volunteer sit down for coffee. She is still upset.

The issue: Do you help the volunteer understand the child and breach confidentiality OR keep quiet and risk her misunderstanding?

Response: You tell. It will help her to work with the child.

IS IT ETHICAL? • 8A

The Nap

The mother of a 4-year-old in your class has asked that he not nap at school, because when he naps he stays up too late at night, making it difficult for her to get up at 5 a.m. to go to work. You think he seems to need his nap to stay in good spirits in the afternoon.

The issue: Do you respect the mother's wishes and wake him up OR do you tell her no because he needs the nap?

Response: You wake him up. The mother knows what her family needs, and you want to support her.

IS IT ETHICAL? • 9A

Cooking with Children

You are a preschool teacher and have just moved to another state and taken a job. You have always included lots of cooking in your curriculum and believe that it is a great way to motivate children and integrate learning. After your first cooking project in your new job, the director takes you aside and tells you that cooking is against licensing rules in this state because of potential health and safety risks to children.

The issue: Do you follow this regulation even though you believe it's stupid and wrong OR do you do what you believe is best practice?

Response: You stop cooking but complain a lot to the other staff and the parents.

IS IT ETHICAL? • 10A

The Divorce

You are the teacher of a 7-year-old whose parents are going through a very contentious divorce. The mother has been a model parent and always helps out in your class. She seems very loving and concerned. The father often comes into school raging and complaining. He is harsh with his child. You have been asked by the child's mother to testify on her behalf in a child custody hearing.

The issue: Do you agree to testify? Do you take the side of one parent over another in a conflict OR do you remain neutral?

Response: You agree to testify. It's obvious that the mother will be a better parent.

IS IT ETHICAL? • 11A

Cultural Differences

You teach in a school that has a population from a culture in which physical punishment is common. This morning a boy from this cultural group strikes another child. A new aide who shares the child's culture grabs him and twists his ear. The child is momentarily stunned but soon is fine and seems calm the rest of the day. Apart from some redness, there are no other effects. When you speak with the aide, she tells you children in her community are used to this discipline. She says, "It calmed him down, didn't it?"

The issue: Do you tell the aide that physical punishment is not acceptable in your class OR do you let it go?

Response: You let it go because she knows the culture better than you do.

IS IT ETHICAL? • 12A

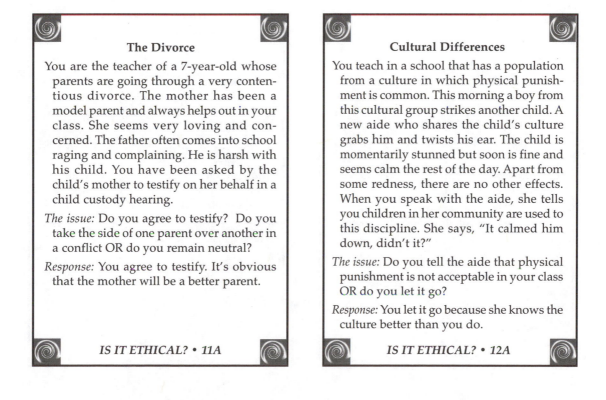

Contagious Diarrhea

You have been informed that a 2-year old in the next classroom has been diagnosed as having contagious diarrhea. You expect families will be alerted to the illness through a posted notice, but the director of your center has dismissed the problem, only telling teachers to be sure to wear gloves and wash their hands after changing the child. You go to the director and express your concern. She says she doesn't want to upset the parents and that good hygiene should take care of the problem.

The issue: Do you tell parents or the board of directors of the situation and your concern OR do you assume the director knows what she's doing?

Response: You don't tell; you're afraid that she'll get angry and this will make your work situation unpleasant.

IS IT ETHICAL? • 13A

Going Home

You are a kindergarten teacher. One student's mother comes to pick up her child and drive him home. From her slurred speech and clumsy movements, you suspect that she has been drinking heavily after work.

The issue: Do you refuse to let the parent take the child and ask her to call someone else to drive OR do you let her drive the child home?

Response: You decide to ignore it this time, because you're not sure that she's really drunk.

IS IT ETHICAL? • 14A

The Harsh Teacher

The teacher in the next room has always been brusque with the children. Lately, however you are becoming increasingly concerned about her open hostility and harshness toward children. You have seen her shake a child and heard her belittle a child.

The issue: Do you confront the teacher about her harsh behavior OR do you ignore it?

Response: You ask to meet with her one day after school and tell her about your concerns.

IS IT ETHICAL? • 15A

The Ethnic Joke

You teach in a preschool. One afternoon in the lounge, you hear a co-worker make an insulting joke about children and families of a particular ethnic group. It makes you feel uncomfortable, and you think her comments show an unhealthy prejudice. But everyone else laughs.

The issue: Do you risk losing your good relationship with your colleague by saying something OR do you try to ignore it?

Response: You are silent. It would be too embarrassing to confront them.

IS IT ETHICAL? • 16A

Feeney, Freeman, and Moravcik

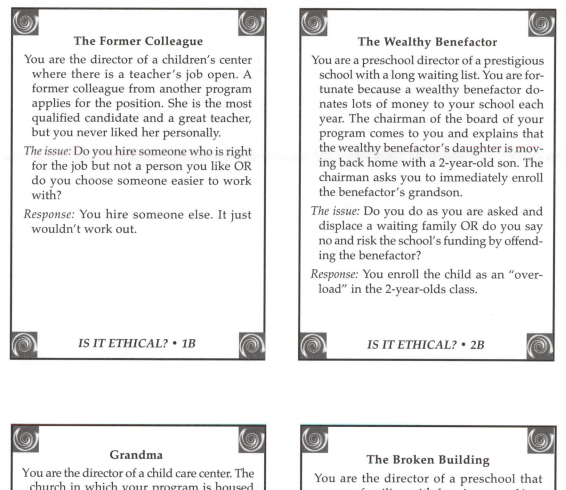

The Former Colleague

You are the director of a children's center where there is a teacher's job open. A former colleague from another program applies for the position. She is the most qualified candidate and a great teacher, but you never liked her personally.

The issue: Do you hire someone who is right for the job but not a person you like OR do you choose someone easier to work with?

Response: You hire someone else. It just wouldn't work out.

IS IT ETHICAL? • *1B*

The Wealthy Benefactor

You are a preschool director of a prestigious school with a long waiting list. You are fortunate because a wealthy benefactor donates lots of money to your school each year. The chairman of the board of your program comes to you and explains that the wealthy benefactor's daughter is moving back home with a 2-year-old son. The chairman asks you to immediately enroll the benefactor's grandson.

The issue: Do you do as you are asked and displace a waiting family OR do you say no and risk the school's funding by offending the benefactor?

Response: You enroll the child as an "overload" in the 2-year-olds class.

IS IT ETHICAL? • *2B*

Grandma

You are the director of a child care center. The church in which your program is housed has decided to sponsor adult day care for the elderly. To make room, you will have to close a classroom, reduce enrollment, and lay off staff. You have two choices. You can lay off "Grandma," who is loved by parents and has been with the center for many years. Grandma is only minimally competent by today's standards and does not have training or credentials. Your other choice is to lay off the teacher hired most recently. She is young, well trained, and does a good job in the classroom.

The issue: Do you lay off a more competent and qualified teacher OR the one who is only marginally competent?

Response: You keep Grandma on. The younger teacher will find another job.

IS IT ETHICAL? • *3B*

The Broken Building

You are the director of a preschool that serves families with low incomes. Your rent is very low, which allows you to charge a very low tuition to families. Your landlord has let the building fall into dangerous disrepair. There are no other low-rent facilities in the community.

The issue: Do you move to a safer, more expensive facility and raise tuition, forcing some families out of care, OR do you make the best of it and keep tuition low?

Response: You stay! Families desperately need your program. You and the staff watch the children carefully to make sure that no one gets hurt.

IS IT ETHICAL? • *4B*

Gossip

You are a preschool director. One day you go to a classroom to give a teacher a message. It's naptime, and you observe two teachers discussing the home life of a child whose father has been arrested for drunk driving.

The issue: Do you tell the teachers that this is not acceptable behavior OR do you let it go and maintain your relationship with the teachers?

Response: You tell them to stop. You can't let gossip flourish in your school.

IS IT ETHICAL? • 5B

The Former Employee

You are a preschool director who hears through the grapevine that a former employee was charged with abusing her own child but was acquitted. You receive a call from another director who says that the former employee has given your name as a reference and she is considering hiring her.

The issue: Do you only share information about her work with you OR do you mention the child abuse charge even though she was acquitted?

Response: You only share what you know through direct experience.

IS IT ETHICAL? • 6B

The Ineffective CPS Agency

You are the director of a child care center. A child in your center shows definite signs of being abused. You know that you should report the case to your local child protective services agency. But the last time you referred a child to them, a worker visited the family but did not promptly intervene. The family left town, never to be heard from again.

The issue: Do you report your suspicion even though you think it may have negative consequences for the child OR do you try to intervene in other ways?

Response: You decide not to file a report and instead contact the minister of the family's church to get help.

IS IT ETHICAL? • 7B

The Academic Curriculum

You are a center director and have been approached by the corporation that runs your program and asked to use a highly academic curriculum that takes up most of each morning. This makes you very uncomfortable. Your continued good relationship with your employer and possibly your job are dependent on your agreeing to this request.

The issue: Do you agree even though you do not believe that this is in the best interests of children OR do you refuse and risk your job?

Response: You agree, you can't afford to lose your job right now.

IS IT ETHICAL? • 8B

Feeney, Freeman, and Moravcik

(**E**=Ethical, **NE**=Not Ethical)

Situation 1A—The Broken Marriage. **NE.** P-2.9: We shall maintain confidentiality and shall respect the family's right to privacy, ...

Situation 2A—The Bed Wetter. **NE.** P-1.6: When we have reasonable cause to suspect child abuse or neglect, we shall report it to the appropriate community agency . . . .

Situation 3A—The Great Assistant. **NE.** P-3A.2: We shall exercise care in expressing views regarding the personal attributes or professional conduct of co-workers. Statements should be based on firsthand knowledge and relevant to the interest of children and programs. (Participants might also mention I-3A.3: To support co-workers in meeting their professional needs and in their professional development; and I-3A.4: To accord co-workers due recognition of professional achievement.)

Situation 4A—The Aggressive Child. **NE.** P-1.4: For every child we shall implement adaptations . . . consult with the family, and seek recommendations from appropriate specialists to maximize the potential of the child to benefit from the program. If, after these efforts have been made to work with a child and family, the child does not appear to be benefiting from a program . . . we shall communicate with the family and appropriate specialists to determine the child's current needs. . . .

Situation 5A—The Incompetent Teacher. **NE.** P-3A.1: When we have a concern about the professional behavior of a co-worker, we shall first let that person know of our concern, ... P-4.6: We shall report the unethical or incompetent behavior of a colleague to a supervisor when informal resolution is not effective.

Situation 6A—HIV/AIDS. **E.** P-1.2: We shall not participate in practices that discriminate against children. . . . P-2.2: We shall inform families of program philosophy, policies. . . .

Situation 7A—The High-Paying Job. **E.**: P-3B.1: When we do not agree with program policies, we shall first attempt to effect change through constructive action within the organization.

Situation 8A—The Volunteer. **NE.** P-2.9: We shall maintain confidentiality and shall respect the family's right to privacy. . . .

Situation 9A—The Nap. *It depends:* **E**, if we determine that it is not harmful to the child. I-2.4: To respect families' childrearing values and their right to make decisions for their children. **NE,** if we determine that it is harmful to the child to be deprived of a nap. P.1.1: Above all, we shall not harm children. We shall not participate in practices that are harmful to children. *This principle has precedence over all others in this Code.*

Situation 10A—Cooking with Children. **E.** P-4.8: We shall not participate in practices which are in violation of laws and regulations that protect children in our programs. This teacher might also consider I-4.6: To support policies and laws that promote the well-being of children and families, and to oppose those that impair their well-being. To participate in developing policies and laws that are needed. . . .

Situation 11A—The Divorce. **NE.** P-2.10: In cases where family members are in conflict, we shall work openly, sharing our observations of the child, to help all parties. . . . We shall refrain from becoming an advocate for one party.

Situation 12A—Cultural Differences. **NE.** P-3A.1: When we have a concern about the professional behavior of a co-worker, we shall first let that person know of our concern, ... P-4.6: We shall report the unethical or incompetent behavior of a colleague to a supervisor when informal resolution is not effective.

Situation 13A—Contagious Diarrhea. **NE.** P-2.5: We shall inform the family of risks such as exposures to contagious disease that may result in infection. P-3B.1: When we do not agree with program policies, we shall first attempt to effect change through constructive action within the organization. P-4.9: When we have evidence that an early childhood program is violating laws or regulations protecting children, we shall report it to persons responsible for the program.

Situation 14A—Going Home. *It depends*: **NE,** if you think the mother's driving might endanger the child. P-1.1: Above all, we shall not harm children. We shall not participate in practices. . . . **E,** if you think that you have no right to intervene in a family decision. I-2.4: To respect families' childrearing values and their right to make decisions for their children. (This situation depends on how you interpret your responsibilities under P-1.1).

Situation 15A—The Harsh Teacher. **NE.** P-3A.1 and P-4.6: We shall report the unethical or incompetent behavior of a colleague to a supervisor when informal resolution is not effective.

Situation 16A—The Ethnic Joke. **NE.** P-3A.1: When we have a concern about the professional behavior of a co-worker, we shall first let that person know of our concern, ... (Participants might also mention I-2.3: To respect the dignity of each family and its culture, language, customs, and beliefs.)

Feeney, Freeman, and Moravcik

Master Sheet — Set B
Administrator Focus

(E=Ethical; **NE**=Not Ethical)

Situation 1B—The Former Colleague. **NE.** P-3C.7: Hiring and promotion shall be based solely on a person's record of accomplishment and ability to carry out the responsibilities of the position.

Situation 2B—The Wealthy Benefactor. **NE.** P-1.2: We shall not participate in practices that discriminate against children by denying benefits, giving special advantages, ...

Situation 3B—Grandma. **NE.** P-3C.6: In making evaluations and recommendations, judgments shall be based on fact and relevant to the interests of children and programs.

Situation 4B—The Broken Building. *It depends:* **E,** if you feel that the condition of the building endangers children engaged in typical play. P-1.1: Above all we shall not harm children. . . . not participate in practices that are . . . dangerous . . . . **NE,** if you do not think the condition of the building endangers children. (Note: There are a number of ways to finesse this problem on behalf of children and families, such as fundraising, grant-writing, work days, and negotiation with the landlord.)

Situation 5B—Gossip. **E.** P-3C.4: Employees who do not meet program standards shall be informed of areas of concern. . . .

Situation 6B—The Former Employee. **E.** P-3C.6: In making evaluations and recommendations, judgments shall be based on fact and relevant to the interests of children and programs. (You state that your comments only give information that is relevant to the position and based on your experience of the person's work.)

Situation 7B—The Ineffective CPS Agency. *It depends:* **NE,** if you think you can do something to assure that the child will be adequately protected if you make the referral. P-1.5 . . . We shall know and follow state laws . . . that protect children against abuse and neglect. **E,** if you believe that child is in danger of serious harm and you can find an alternative source of protection. P-1.1: Above all, we shall not harm children. . . .

Situation 8B—The Academic Curriculum. *It depends:* **NE,** if you do not believe that the new program is harmful to children. **E,** if you believe that the program will be harmful to children. P-1.1: Above all, we shall not harm children . . . . (Participants may mention I-1.2: To base program practices upon current knowledge in the field of child development . . . .)

References

Bebeau, M.J. 1993. Designing an outcome-based ethics curriculum for professional education: Strategies and evidence of effectiveness. *Journal of Moral Education* 22 (3): 313–26.

Brophy-Herb, H., L.C. Stein, & M. Kostelnik. 1998. Ethical explorations: Highlighting ethics in teacher training. Paper presented at the NAEYC Annual Conference, Toronto, Ontario, Canada, November 1998.

Fasoli, L., & C. Woodrow. 1991. *Getting ethical: A resource book for workshop leaders*. Australian Early Childhood Education Resource Booklets. Vol. 3. Watson, ACT: Australian Early Childhood Association.

Feeney, S., D. Christensen, & E. Moravcik. 1996. *Instructor's manual to accompany "Who am I in the lives of children?"* 5th ed. Columbus, OH: Merrill.

Feeney, S., & N.K. Freeman. 1999. *Ethics and the early childhood educator: Using the NAEYC Code.* Washington, DC: NAEYC.

Feeney, S., & K. Kipnis. 1985. Professional ethics in early childhood education. *Young Children* 40 (3): 54–58.

Feeney, S., & K. Kipnis. 1998. *Code of ethical conduct and statement of commitment.* Rev. ed. Washington, DC: NAEYC.

Freeman, N.K. 1996. Professional ethics: A survey of early childhood teacher educators and a curriculum for preservice teachers. Ph.D. diss., College of Education, University of South Carolina, Columbia.

Freeman, N.K. 1997. Using NAEYC's Code of Ethics: Mama and Daddy taught me right from wrong—Isn't that enough? *Young Children* 52 (6): 64–67.

Freeman, N.K. 2000. Protecting adults and children from blood-borne pathogens. *Dimensions of Early Childhood* 28 (2): 8–16.

Freeman, N.K., & M.H. Brown. 1996. Ethics instruction for preservice teachers: How are we doing in ECE? *Journal of Early Childhood Teacher Education* 17 (2): 5–18.

Griffen, S., & F. Ricks. n.d. *Taking right action: A facilitator's manual to the "Early Childhood Educators of British Columbia code of ethics."* Vancouver, BC, Canada: Early Childhood Educators of British Columbia.

Hostetler, K.D., & B.S. Hostetler. 1997. *Ethical judgment in teaching.* Boston: Allyn & Bacon.

Kidder, R.M. 1995. *How good people make tough choices: Resolving the dilemmas of ethical living.* New York: Fireside.

NAEYC Ethics Panel. 1995. How many ways can you think of to use NAEYC's Code of Ethics? *Young Children* 51 (1): 42–43.

Newman, L., & L. Pollnitz. 1999. *Will my response be ethical? A reflective process to guide the practice of early childhood students and professionals.* (Instructor's manual also available by the same title.) Sydney, Australia: Committee for University Teaching and Staff Development.

Nolte, S. 1998. *PACE (Professional and Career Education for Early Childhood) training manual for ED 140.* Rev. ed. Honolulu, Hawaii: Honolulu Community College.

Stonehouse, A. 1994. *Not just nice ladies.* Castle Hill, NSW, Australia: Pademelon.

Wasserman, S. 1994. *Introduction to case method teaching: A guide to the galaxy.* New York: Teachers College Press.

Recommended Reading Resources

    This list of resources will give you additional background to help you teach about ethics and the NAEYC Code of Ethical Conduct. The first set of resources includes references about ethics and professionalism (reprinted from *Ethics and the Early Childhood Educator*). The other two sets contain a selection of recommended books about teaching adults and about teaching with cases.

Ethics and professionalism

Gilligan, Carol. 1982. *In a different voice.* Cambridge, MA: Harvard University Press.
  A groundbreaking and influential work that describes women's moral development.

Hostetler, K.D., & B.S. Hostetler. 1997. *Ethical judgment in teaching.* Boston: Allyn & Bacon.
  This resource models ethical problem solving and highlights the importance of developing the ability to think and speak clearly as you consider ethical dilemmas.

Katz, L.G. 1995. *Talks with teachers of young children: A collection.* Norwood, NJ: Ablex.
  These essays, originally published between 1977 and 1985, are foundational works that have given focus to and paved the way for much of the work done in the field of ethics in early childhood education. See particularly Chapter 11, The professional preschool teacher; Chapter 14, The nature of professions: Where is early childhood education; and Chapter 15, Ethical issues in working with young children.

Kidder, R.M. 1995. *How good people make tough choices: Resolving the dilemmas of ethical living.* New York: Fireside.
  A clear and easy-to-understand primer. A good place to begin your study of ethics and ethical decisionmaking.

Kipnis, K. 1987. How to discuss professional ethics. *Young Children* 42 (4): 26–30.
  Kipnis's definitions and advice have guided our profession's conversations about ethics from the beginning of the field's discussion of this important topic.

Nash, R.J. 1996. *"Real world" ethics: Frameworks for educators and human service professionals.* New York: Teachers College Press.
  A reader-friendly theoretical book that considers how those in the service professions approach ethical dilemmas by melding their personal morality and character with professional ethics to guide their problem-solving efforts.

Noddings, N. 1984. *Caring: A feminine approach to ethics and moral education.* Berkeley: University of California Press.

A benchmark work that explores characteristics of caring relationships that are at the heart of our work with young children and their families.

Strike, K.A., & J.F. Soltis, eds. 1992. *The ethics of teaching.* 2d ed. New York: Teachers College Press.

A basic resource for students examining ethical issues in education. Strike and Soltis apply ethical theories to teachers' work and model ethical decisionmaking.

Strike, K.A., & P.L. Ternasky, eds. 1993. *Ethics for professionals in education: Perspectives for education and practice.* New York: Teachers College Press.

A valuable resource for readers who are eager to explore moral theory and the dynamics and implications of educators' moral decisionmaking.

See also the "Using the NAEYC Code of Ethics" articles that are frequently featured in *Young Children.*

Teaching adults

Belenky, M.F., B. Clinchy, N. Goldberger, & J.M. Tarule. 1997. *Women's ways of knowing: The development of self, voice and mind.* 10th anniversary ed. New York: Basic.

A foundational book that describes how women understand truth, knowledge, and authority and how they make sense of their experiences.

Carter, M., & D. Curtis. 1994. *Training teachers: A harvest of theory and practice.* Minnesota: Redleaf.

Suggestions for teaching teachers in ways that allow them to construct their own knowledge and respect their own learning styles so they can help children do the same.

Freiberg, H.J., & A. Driscoll. 2000. *Universal teaching strategies.* 3rd ed. Boston: Allyn & Bacon.

Presents strategies for organizing, implementing, and assessing teaching. Each section cuts across grade levels, subject areas, and teaching situations.

Jones, E. 1986. *Teaching adults: An active learning approach.* Washington, DC: NAEYC.

Suggestions for teaching adults using the kinds of active learning approaches that are used in teaching children.

Jones, E., ed. 1993. *Growing teachers: Partnerships in staff training.* Washington, DC: NAEYC.

Suggestions for staff development. Individuals and mentors share stories through stories of their satisfying personal journeys toward effective teaching.

Vella, J. 1997. *Learning to listen, learning to teach: The power of dialogue in educating adults.* San Francisco: Jossey-Bass.

Demonstrates how to apply the principles of adult learning theory when teaching groups of adults.

Yankelovich, D. 1999. *The magic of dialogue: Transforming conflict into cooperation.* New York: Simon & Schuster.

Describes 15 strategies to promote and sustain effective problem-solving communication.

Teaching with cases

Colbert, J.A., P. Desberg, & K. Trimble, eds. 1995. *The case for education: Contemporary approaches for using case methods.* Boston: Allyn & Bacon.

Leaders in the field describe their effective and innovative uses of cases. Includes stories authors have used effectively with a variety of students.

Driscoll, A. 1995. *Cases in early childhood education: Stories of programs and practices.* Boston: Allyn & Bacon.

Chapter-length descriptions of developmentally appropriate classrooms and reflective teaching that are helpful for instructors who want students to envision how the concepts, strategies, and issues they teach about look in practice.

Isenberg, J., & M.R. Jalongo. 1995. *Teachers' stories: From personal narrative to professional insight.* San Francisco: Jossey-Bass.

Shows how teacher educators can use stories of professional experiences to help teachers reflect on their practice. It offers strategies for generating, sharing, and using narratives.

Merseth, K.K. 1991. *The case for cases in teacher education.* Washington, DC: American Association of Colleges of Teacher Education. (Also available as an ERIC document, ED 329541.)

Makes the point that cases are central to teacher education, not an add-on but a cornerstone to help teachers become problem solvers who can apply theory to real-life situations.

Rand, M.K. 2000. *Giving it some thought: Cases for early childhood practice.* Washington, DC: NAEYC.

Offers 49 real examples to help teachers-in-training start thinking as decisionmakers. As they work with these cases, students wrestle with tough issues and gain experience and strategies for thinking through difficult situations.

Shulman, J.H., ed. 1992. *Case methods in teacher education.* New York: Teachers College Press.

Describes effective uses of cases for a variety of instructional purposes. Just one of this expert's resources that introduce and support teachers in using cases to teach adults.

Wasserman, S. 1993. *Getting down to cases: Learning to teach with case studies.* New York: Teachers College Press.

Guides college teachers learning to using case method teaching to promote lively student discussions in examining critical incidents in the classroom.

Wasserman, S. 1994. *Introduction to case method teaching: A guide to the galaxy.* New York: Teachers College Press.

Introduces teaching with cases and offers advice to help teachers of adults successfully implement case method teaching.

Online Sources
for Codes of Ethics

Ethical codes can be found on the Websites of many organizations. Try an organization's acronym plus *.org*. Codes are often found under the heading of Position Statements. The easiest way to locate them is to search for *ethics* within the organization's Website.

Following are links to ethical codes of some helping professions that should be useful in Activities 14, 15, and 16 on codes of ethics in Part 2, second section "Teaching the NAEYC Code." (We do not include links to the codes for doctors and lawyers, because these are extremely detailed and address many issues not relevant to early childhood education.)

Association for Child and Youth Care Practice (ACYCP)
Code of Ethics: Standards for Practice of North American Child and
Youth Care Professionals (1998)
www.acycp.org/codeof.htm

Australia Early Childhood Association (AECA)
Ethics offerings include a code (1990), books, and posters.
www.aeca.org.au/code.html

Council for Exceptional Children (CEC)
Code of Ethics for Educators of Persons with Exceptionalities (1993)
www.cec.sped.org/ps/code.htm#1

Early Childhood Development Association of Prince Edward Island
Early Childhood Development Association of P.E.I. Code of Ethics (n.d.)
www.cfc-efc.ca/ecdapei/code.htm

Early Childhood Educators of British Columbia
www.cfc-efc.ca/ecebc/public.htm

Feeney, Freeman, and Moravcik

Idaho Department of Education
Code of Ethics of the Idaho Teaching Profession (1996)
www.sde.state.id.us/certification/CertMan/certapp_A.htm

National Association for the Education of Young Children (NAEYC)
Code of Ethical Conduct and Statement of Commitment, rev. ed. (1998)
www.naeyc.org/about/position/pseth98.htm

National Association of Biology Teachers
Ethics Statement for Biology Teachers (1985)
www.nabt.org/ethics.html

National Association of Elementary School Principals (NAESP)
Statement of Ethics for School Administrators (1997)
www.naesp.org/ethics.htm

National Council for the Social Studies (NCSS)
Revised Code of Ethics for the Social Studies Profession (1990)
www.ncss.org/standards/positions/ethics.html

National Education Association (NEA)
Code of Ethics of the Education Profession (1975)
www.nea.org/aboutnea/code.html

North Carolina Public Schools
Code of Professional Practice and Conduct for North Carolina
Educators (1997)
www.dpi.state.nc.us/teacher_education/conductcode.htm

Information about NAEYC

NAEYC is . . .

an organization of nearly 102,000 members, founded in 1926, that is committed to fostering the growth and development of children from birth through age 8. Membership is open to all who share a desire to serve young children and act on behalf of the needs and rights of all children.

NAEYC provides . . .

educational services and resources to adults and programs working with and for children, including

• *Young Children, the* peer-reviewed journal for early childhood educators

• **Books, posters, brochures, position statements, and videos** to expand your knowledge and commitment and support your work with young children and families, including such topics as inclusion, diversity, literacy, guidance, assessment, developmentally appropriate practice, and teaching

• **An Annual Conference,** the largest education conference in North America, that brings people together from across the United States and other countries to share their expertise and advocate on behalf of children and families

• **Week of the Young Child** celebrations planned annually by NAEYC Affiliate Groups in communities around the country to call public attention to the critical significance of the child's early years

• **Insurance plans** for members and programs

• **Public affairs information,** and access to information through NAEYC resources and communication systems, for conducting knowledgeable advocacy efforts at all levels of government and in the media

• **A voluntary accreditation system** for high-quality programs for children through the National Academy of Early Childhood Programs

• **Professional development resources and programs** through the National Institute for Early Childhood Professional Development, working to improve the quality and consistency of early childhood preparation and leadership opportunities

• **Young Children International** to promote international communication, discussion forums, and information exchanges

For information about membership, publications, or other NAEYC services, visit NAEYC online at **www.naeyc.org**

National Association for the Education of Young Children
1509 16th Street, NW, Washington, DC 20036-1426
202-232-8777 or 800-424-2460